"This book is a must-read for anyone who wants a healthier relationship with food. Our 'druggified' food supply makes us all vulnerable to the problem of compulsive overconsumption. This practical guide, informed by the latest science and decades of clinical experience, is a tutorial in self-compassion as much as a science-help approach to overeating. I highly recommend."

—**Anna Lembke, MD**, *New York Times* bestselling author of *Dopamine Nation*

"Pretty much every bad thing you've heard about what ultra-processed foods (UPFs) can do to you is true. How to defend yourself? That answer—in expert, actionable detail—is found in this book."

—**David L. Katz, MD, MPH**, past president of the American College of Lifestyle Medicine, and founder of True Health Initiative

"Claire Wilcox has expertly woven together the wisdom of academics and clinicians in the field with her own knowledge to produce an essential guide to the topic of addiction to UPFs. The book is a concise distillation of the current research and treatment options for understanding this complex condition. I will definitely be recommending this book to colleagues and professionals alike."

—**Jen Unwin, PsyD**, clinical health psychologist, and author of *Fork in the Road*

"If you, your loved ones, or your clients struggle with addictive eating, this book is a must-read. Grounded in science and research, Claire Wilcox synthesizes and summarizes a massive amount of information into a clear, personal, and engaging guide that will show you how to move forward. Addressing the neuroscience, nutrition, and complexities when there are eating disorders present, she leaves no stone unturned."

—**Susan Peirce Thompson, PhD**, professor of brain and cognitive sciences, and *New York Times* bestselling author of *Bright Line Eating*

"An insightful and empowering guide to breaking free from food addiction, this book combines cutting-edge neuroscience with practical strategies to help rewire your brain and reclaim control over your eating habits. A must-read for anyone seeking lasting change."

—**Nicole Avena, PhD**, author of *Sugarless*

"Wilcox truly understands the nuance of addiction-like eating and the range of treatment approaches available. She wrote this masterpiece to help you discover what recovery and freedom can be."

—**David Wiss, PhD**, mental health nutritionist, founder of Nutrition in Recovery, and creator of the Wise Mind Nutrition app

"A very important, scientifically based contribution to understanding and treating food addiction which does an exemplary job at bridging the gap between theory and practice. This is as much a groundbreaking self-help book as it is an essential guide for medical practitioners and mental health providers treating obesity and eating disorders."

—**David Aaron Kessler, MD**, pediatrician, attorney, former commissioner of the Food and Drug Administration (FDA), and *New York Times* bestselling author of *The End of Overeating*

"What a compassionate, scholarly, and immensely readable book. It beautifully bridges the gap between the complex worlds of neuroscience, clinical medicine, and lived experience. Essential reading for anyone who feels like they have an addicted relationship with food."

—**Chris van Tulleken, PhD, MD**, associate professor at University College London, author of *Ultra-Processed People*, and radio and television broadcaster and documentarian

REWIRE YOUR FOOD-ADDICTED BRAIN

Fight Cravings and Break Free from a High-Sugar, Ultra-Processed Diet Using Neuroscience

CLAIRE WILCOX, MD

New Harbinger Publications, Inc.

Publisher's Note

This publication is designed to provide accurate and authoritative information in regard to the subject matter covered. It is sold with the understanding that the publisher is not engaged in rendering psychological, financial, legal, or other professional services. If expert assistance or counseling is needed, the services of a competent professional should be sought.

NEW HARBINGER PUBLICATIONS is a registered trademark of New Harbinger Publications, Inc.

New Harbinger Publications is an employee-owned company.

Copyright © 2025 by Claire Wilcox
New Harbinger Publications, Inc.
5720 Shattuck Avenue
Oakland, CA 94609
www.newharbinger.com

All Rights Reserved

Cover design by Amy Daniel

Acquired by Jed Bickman

Edited by Rebecca Job

Library of Congress Cataloging-in-Publication Data on file

Printed in the United States of America

27	26	25							
10	9	8	7	6	5	4	3	2	1

First Printing

Contents

Foreword — v

Introduction — 1

PART 1: The Science of Food Addiction

Chapter 1 Is Food Really Addictive? — 8

Chapter 2 Which Foods Are Problematic? — 21

Chapter 3 The Neurobiology of Overeating: The Homeostatic and Hedonic Systems — 32

Chapter 4 The Stress Response System — 42

Chapter 5 Addiction as a Disorder of Decision Making — 51

PART 2: Diagnosis, Treatment, and Recovery

Chapter 6 Diagnosis and Assessment — 62

Chapter 7 The Sacrifice Is the Promise — 76

Chapter 8 What To Eat? Food Plans — 87

Chapter 9 How to Eat: Abstinence versus Harm Reduction — 110

Chapter 10 Skills to Reduce Food Cue Sensitivity — 120

Chapter 11 Skills to Enhance Emotional Resilience — 132

Chapter 12 Skills to Improve Decision Making — 143

Conclusion — 149

Acknowledgments — 151

References — 153

Foreword

As hosts of the *Food Junkies Podcast*, it is a true honor to introduce this groundbreaking book by Dr. Wilcox. Our podcast has been a labor of love, dedicated to exploring the complex and often misunderstood world of food addiction. Through our interviews and discussions, we've aimed to offer hope, support, and practical insights to those struggling with this challenging condition. When Dr. Wilcox approached us with the idea of using our podcast as a foundation for this comprehensive guide, we were immediately excited by the potential impact it could have on the lives of our listeners and beyond.

For years, we have poured our efforts into raising awareness about ultra-processed food addiction. We have interviewed leading experts, shared compelling personal stories, and delved into cutting-edge research, all with the goal of helping people understand this multifaceted issue. This book takes that mission a step further, transforming the wealth of knowledge we've accumulated into a resource that is both accessible and deeply rooted in science. It is a reflection of the conversations and revelations we've shared on the podcast, but now in a format that can be easily referenced and revisited.

What makes this book particularly special is its ability to bridge the often-intimidating gap between academic research and real-world application. Dr. Wilcox has skillfully taken insights from our podcast guests, current scientific literature, and proven recovery strategies to create a guide that not only explains the neurobiology of food addiction but also provides a practical roadmap for those seeking to overcome it. This book doesn't just inform; it empowers readers to take control of their relationship with food, offering both education and actionable steps for sustainable recovery.

We strongly support incorporating nutrition-focused treatments into recovery programs, as nourishing both the brain and body is essential for true healing. Many people who seek support within traditional eating disorder frameworks often find their symptoms worsening, underscoring the need for a more tailored approach. By fostering collaboration between eating disorder and food addiction professionals, we can build a unified, compassionate approach that better supports recovery and promotes a healthier, stigma-free society.

Our mission is also to raise awareness about ultra-processed food addiction in the deeper hope of breaking down the stigma surrounding all forms of addiction. Many of us experience challenges with these highly engineered foods, and recognizing this universal struggle can foster empathy and understanding toward those facing other forms of addiction. For those who feel alone in their struggle, acknowledging food addiction can be a first step toward reducing shame and seeking support without fear of judgment.

We believe this book will become an essential resource for anyone touched by ultra-processed food addiction, whether personally or professionally. Its comprehensive yet approachable style ensures that readers will find it both enlightening and applicable to their own lives. We are truly honored to have played a role in its creation through our podcast, and we are excited to see the transformative power it will have on the journey to recovery.

—Vera Tarman, Clarissa Kennedy, and Molly Painschab,
hosts of the *Food Junkies Podcast*

Introduction

"Willfully addictive hyperpalatable junk foods are engineered toxins."

—David Katz, *Food Junkies Podcast*

Most of the food products that flood our grocery shelves today are processed to the hilt, designed by Big Food to make us want more and more. Instead of selling foods in their natural form, the food industry crafts their products with the goal of creating addiction in mind. The end result: we get hooked, developing intense cravings and deeply entrenched, unhelpful habits around certain foods. If you're one of these people, this book will show you a path toward freeing yourself.

The global increase in chronic conditions like diabetes, metabolic syndrome, and obesity can be traced back to the food industry and a lack of regulation to curb its undue influence. In the 1960s, Big Food began engineering their products to enhance taste. The more rewarding the product, the more people craved, and the more they kept buying it—simple economics. People started to gain weight, and the problem fed itself.

Michael Moss, Pulitzer Prize-winning investigative reporter and author of *Hooked*, appeared on the *Food Junkies Podcast* to discuss what happens behind the scenes in the food industry. He described how scientists and engineers in industry laboratories design their products to enhance qualities like "craveability," "bliss point," and "vanishing caloric density," which refers to how ultra-processed foods are crafted to dissolve in your mouth so fast that your brain doesn't realize it ate anything at all. Ultra-processed food, Moss says, is in many ways the "new tobacco," and "many of these food products are even more problematic and more addictive than even some of the harsher [addictive] drugs" (Moss 2021).

The new tobacco, indeed. In the 1980s, tobacco company R.J. Reynolds purchased Nabisco, then sold it to Philip Morris—which also bought General Foods and Kraft, thus becoming the single largest manufacturer of processed food in North America. Big Tobacco became Big Food. To make things worse, the food industry has meddled behind the scenes, funding biased academic research and influencing medical and nutritionist education to downplay the numerous negative health consequences of sugar and ultra-processed foods.

The public continues to be misled. Much of food advertising targets children, who give a lifetime of profit potential. Food industry giants now own Weight Watchers, Jenny Craig, and SlimFast, which tout ineffective calorie reduction models and dress up ultra-processed foods as healthy and market them. Screens (television, computers, smartphones) are used to condition our behavior and feed our need for their products.

The Problem

Thanks to a growing body of research, it's now nearly impossible to refute: high-sugar, ultra-processed foods are addictive. Just like nicotine, alcohol, and other drugs of abuse, they light up our reward centers and create troughs in our brain. In those of us who are susceptible—either due to genetics, overexposure to sugary ultra-processed foods at a young age, trauma, or other factors outside of our control—these foods, over time, have rewired our brains, driving them to prefer the factory-made food that many of us instinctively find hyperpalatable (Wilcox 2021).

The core symptoms of food addiction are cravings, obsessions, and compulsions to overeat foods that are heavily processed and/or contain a lot of sugar. If you have out-of-control cravings, a tendency to eat certain processed foods to excess, or negative health and emotional consequences from your eating patterns, and find that despite multiple attempts to change, the obsessions and compulsions to return to old eating behaviors just keep coming back, it's possible you have food addiction. I certainly believe I do.

Those of us who are in the throes of food addiction battle constant urges to eat. The obsession wears us down, then in a moment of weakness, we are seduced back into a behavior we were trying to avoid, undermining our most wholesome intentions for ourselves. Yo-yo dieting, weight fluctuations, and poor mental and physical health are the inevitable result. We blame ourselves, believing that it's a problem rooted in our own deficient willpower. Those around us—our friends, family, and doctors—do little to counter these toxic beliefs, and our self-esteem plummets further. We think that we just need to eat less and exercise more, and just break away from our microwaves, computers, and TV screens. We try to change, and we do it over and over, but our commitments never seem to last. We suffer in silence, demoralized and despondent.

The Solution

The good news is that because we now know that food addiction is a biological problem—rooted in our brain and caused by a substance that exists outsides of ourselves—there's a workable, biologically-based solution to get free that's rooted in neuroscience. You can rewire your brain back to health. It also means if you have food addiction, it's not your fault.

First, you will learn how cutting back on the foods that have caused you problems in the first place—namely high-sugar, ultra-processed foods—is a key part of the solution, as it will restore the brain chemistry that was disrupted by these foods in the first place. Your brain has been made sick by these foods. By avoiding them, your brain's sensitivity to food cues, stress resilience, and impulse control will normalize, given time. I'll teach you where and how to draw the line between problem foods and non-problem foods, and how to do it for you as an individual, as we are all different.

You'll also learn additional ways to rewire your brain in a sustainable way so that you can stop and stay stopped, using nutritional, emotional, medical, pharmacological, self-help, spiritual, and psychological tools from eating disorder and addiction models of care. This is key, since as anyone with an addiction will maintain, knowledge and willpower are not enough. For example, you will learn what and how to eat. You'll find out that eating enough delicious, nutritious food is an essential component of restoring your brain's health. You'll get to develop a food plan that works for you, weigh the pros and cons of an abstinence-based approach, and understand important nutritional changes.

We'll explore many additional skills and solutions, which can heal the brain in intentional ways. You'll find out how to build community, rid your environments of food cues, practice self-care, seek therapeutic help, find meaning, consider individualized treatment, and more.

Finally, sometimes people with addictions need supplemental treatment—medication for craving reduction, or treatments for mental health, eating disorders, or other emotional issues. If your case is more complex, the website for this book, http://www.newharbinger.com/54681, has bonus chapters that can guide you through navigating comorbid eating disorders and how to access professional help.

Foundations of This Approach

The content of this book comes from two primary sources. First, the textbook *Food Addiction, Obesity and Disorders of Overeating: An Evidence-Based Assessment and Clinical Guide,* authored and published in 2021 by this book's author, will be frequently referenced; it is a extensively cited work rooted firmly in the academic literature, and evidence-based. It compiles thousands of research studies that firmly establish that food addiction is a real and useful entity.

Second, and perhaps much more importantly, this book is deeply informed and inspired by the *Food Junkies Podcast,* hosted by three women: Vera Tarman, addiction physician and author of the 2019 book *Food Junkies: Recovery From Food Addiction,* an essential and groundbreaking book on food addiction recovery, already in its second edition; and Clarissa Kennedy and Molly Painschab, licensed mental health and addiction clinicians and founders of Sweet Sobriety, a highly successful online treatment program for food addiction. This book draws direct insight from the many food addiction-oriented professionals that have been interviewed on this show, and by doing so presents a consensus, not a personal opinion. Although food addiction is not yet an official diagnosis, behavioral health and health care providers, researchers, investigative reports, historians, nutritionists, eating disorder and addiction specialists, and more have been working and refining their process in the field for decades and are coming to a consensus about the best ways to help people like you get well.

The Desired Outcome

My hope is that if you have food addiction and apply these solutions, you'll benefit in many of the same ways that I and many others with food addiction have experienced. My hope is that you, too, will find release from the insatiable cravings, constant urges, obsessions, and compulsions to eat high-sugar and ultra-processed food to excess. By applying the solutions and skills you are about to learn, you can start eating in a more balanced way and habitually make better food choices, ending the bingeing cycle and the constant exhaustive battle with yourself. You may experience mood improvements as well as better concentration and memory; reduced body pain; and enhanced physical health, vitality, and well-being.

As you'll learn more about in chapter 7, I do not encourage people to make weight loss a primary goal because it can be triggering for many with food addiction. Restrictive eating causes more rebound bingeing. But weight release usually occurs as a result of food addiction recovery, so those of you who want to release weight for health reasons can look forward to that, too. In sum, if all goes well, you'll be done with the misery, and happier and more confident than ever.

What makes this book entirely unique from existing, established solutions is that it is rooted in neuroscience and addresses the problem at its source. It is not a band-aid approach. For those with food addiction, the brain circuitry that drives addictive behavior—including circuits underlying reward, motivation, impulse control, emotion regulation, and habit formation—has been rewired by sugar and ultra-processed foods. The secret to success is nurturing these circuits back to health. You will soon learn how to do exactly that.

PART 1

The Science of Food Addiction

CHAPTER 1

Is Food Really Addictive?

"We have so much evidence that sugar is harmful to health and addictive... that the naysayer's voice has been pretty minimized at this point."

—Nicole Avena, *Food Junkies Podcast*

Maybe it sounds extreme to talk about food as addictive. After all, we have to eat to live, right? And food doesn't make us slur our words, intoxicate us, or cause blackouts, so how can it be grouped in the same category as alcohol and other addictive drugs? We don't go through withdrawal when we stop, do we? Issues with food don't render us penniless, alone, and unrecognizable in the same way that heroin or meth addictions can, right? Or could they?

In this chapter, I will address these questions and more, and by the end, I hope you'll be at least open to the idea that some foods are as addictive and problematic as many of the other substances we find it so easy to brand with that label.

First, you'll learn what "addiction" is. Then you'll learn that some foods (namely high-sugar and ultra-processed food) are more addictive than others, triggering harmful mechanisms in the same way that other addictive substances do—by causing changes in neural circuits that mediate reward, motivation, impulse control, and emotion regulation. Next, I'll teach you about the ways that overexposure to these foods can negatively affect your mental and physical health, including unwanted weight gain and eating disorders.

What Is Addiction?

The word "addiction" is used pretty freely. What does it actually mean? One thing it doesn't mean: enjoyment. That you enjoy eating cookies does not mean at all that you are addicted. Rather, "addiction" centers around a core problem: loss of control.

If you've been addicted to something before, you know what it's like: the obsessive thoughts sneak through the back door of your consciousness while you're guarding the front, leaving their mean-spirited gifts in the form of justifications. These shifts in perspective can be sudden: out of nowhere, it seems like a spectacular idea to use the substance that minutes ago you were convinced was ruining your life. If it's progressed significantly, you still use the substance despite looming disasters and tangible negative consequences. It has taken control of you.

Here are some other descriptions of addiction from a wide range of experts in the field: "a repetitive behavior that some people find difficult to quit" (Moss 2021); "engaging in a reward-driven behavior that's harming them" (Guyenet 2022b); "doing something that you know is wrong, but you can't stop yourself" (Unwin 2021a); a "zombie walk" (Ifland 2021), an "unconscious monster" (Lieberman 2022) and "the toddler in the head" (Lembke 2021a, 2021b). Vera Tarman of Food Junkies also calls it a "multiple personality disorder of behavior" (quoted in Earley 2021). All these descriptions also evoke the core theme of loss of control.

When neuroscientists and researchers use the term "addiction," they too are often referring to a loss of control—one that results from brain changes due to repeated consumption of an addictive substance, or performance of an addictive behavior.

How does this loss of control develop? When we use a substance that makes us feel good in some way, our brain unconsciously learns that it wants more of that substance and pushes us toward consuming the substance again. The more we use and experience benefit from the substance, the more we want to return to it for a similar effect. This learning process is called *associative learning,* and it occurs as a result of a well-mapped-out biological process called *conditioning,* which causes animals and humans to develop habits.

Once conditioning has occurred, many visual, aural, olfactory (smell), and gustatory (taste) memory cues can unconsciously trigger a desire and/or behaviors to seek out and consume a substance. In this way, places we've used a substance before (a bar), seeing items associated with it (beer can), or being exposed to a little bit of it (a taste) can make us want more and more. Similarly, negative mood states that have previously been relieved by substance use will also trigger a similar habitual behavioral response, as can stress. Cues can be *environmental* (outside of ourselves, like a place or a date) or *interoceptive* (inside of ourselves, like an emotion or a memory). Excess substance use—be it drugs, alcohol, nicotine, or sugar-laden processed food—will also affect our impulse control in a more general sense, directly affecting our attention and concentration.

Our vulnerability to these kinds of cues can last long past our last use of the substance, even months or years, although it does diminish over time. The good news, though, is that there are many ways to rewire things back, and to hasten the brain's healing. You'll learn all about them in great detail in part 2.

Is Food Addictive?

Do you know anyone who's cheated on a diet? Rationalized an extra piece of cake when they were trying to be good? Told themselves, "Just tonight," and then went back the next day to the eating behavior they were trying to stop? It's likely that most people, with an honest appraisal of themselves, would say they've experienced loss of control of their eating at some point or another.

For those of us with food addiction, our symptoms are usually more extreme. Sometimes, just a taste of a *trigger food*, or a food that we are particularly vulnerable to overeating, leads to a rampage of feasting: down goes the whole tub of ice cream or a large box of chocolates. In food addiction, the cravings and ingrained habits can become so extreme that they lead to serious, devastating consequences. For us, the loss of control around food can be just as profound as it is for someone with a drug or alcohol problem.

Johnathan Cranford, author of *The Sugar Demons: An Addict's Guide to Conquering Sugar Addiction*, knew he was one of these people when he found himself "staring into my kitchen trash can...looking at 2 empty pints of ice cream":

> I was about to cover them with other trash inside the trash can to hide it and stuff it toward the bottom... I realized in that moment that this isn't normal. Why are you hiding this from your wife and daughter who don't even care?... This isn't what a normal grown man does when he wants to eat ice cream. He doesn't hide his tracks. (Cranford 2021)

Cranford's behavior is eerily similar to what is commonly described by people with other addictions, be it nicotine, alcohol, or heroin. His brain has been conditioned to go into autopilot. His case is extreme, but at some level, do you relate? If so, you might have food addiction, too.

High-Sugar Ultra-Processed Foods Are Especially Addictive

The United States didn't always have a problem with addictive eating. It wasn't until the 1960s that Americans began to consume more calories, and average body weights began to increase. Then in 1997, obesity was declared a global epidemic by the World Health Organization, and today it continues to grow increasingly prevalent. Over 40 percent of adults are now considered obese, according to a 2018 study (Hales et. al. 2020). Studies claim that over one-fifth of deaths in the US are attributable to it, with rates similar to or bypassing smoking (Ward et al. 2022), and obesity is the cause of 10 percent of the national medical budget, or more than $170 billion a year (Ward et al. 2021).

Why have these last decades seen such a significant rise in average body weights? In the early part of the 1900s, we were still eating primarily whole foods from our gardens or directly from animals on our farms. But in the 1960s, ultra-processed foods with high levels of refined carbohydrates (often combined with fat and sugar) flooded our market. These foods are especially addictive.

What are these high-sugar ultra-processed foods I keep referring to? In chapter 2, I'll go into great detail about which foods are addictive and the studies that support this claim. But broadly, this refers to most of the food that's on our grocery store shelves (unfortunately). It's food that has been heavily flavored with additives and emulsifiers, produced in mass quantities in laboratories, and extensively marketed by the food industry. It's usually high in energy density, sodium, sugar, fat, and refined carbohydrates. It has many ingredients (as opposed to a few), fewer favorable micronutrient profiles (*micronutrients* being vitamins and minerals), and macronutrient ratios (i.e., ratios of carbohydrates, fat, and protein) that are nothing like what is seen in foods in their natural states. "High sugar," in particular, means processed foods with added sugar, for which sugar (or one of its many other names) is in the top four listed ingredients.

And why is such food so addictive? Our brains evolved during times of scarcity (in sharp contrast to our present era), when food only minimally activated the reward network. Brains that were more sensitive to food cues and were motivated to consume high-calorie foods when they were available were evolutionarily advantageous. These prehistoric systems are still in our brains, and in today's food environment, the lights in them are going on and off like a pinball machine.

One highly convincing, tightly controlled study in humans found that diets high in ultra-processed food caused 500 calories more a day of food intake over two weeks than those low in ultra-processed food. When the same participants were switched to the opposite experimental group for an additional two weeks, the same finding was seen: those who got ultra-processed food took in more (Hall et al. 2019). This convincing work lends strong support to arguments that ultra-processed foods are largely responsible for the increasing average body weights in industrialized countries.

Ashley Gearhardt, a leading food addiction researcher, addressed the question of food's addictiveness by taking criteria from those used in 1988 by the surgeon general to determine that nicotine was addictive, and adding a fourth (craving). She concluded that ultra-processed food is addictive; it can cause compulsive use, has mood-altering effects, reinforces behavior, and triggers strong urges or craving (Gearhardt and Schulte 2021). If we accept that nicotine is addictive, we must accept that ultra-processed food is addictive too.

True enough, thousands of studies in animal models and human populations show that high-sugar and ultra-processed foods act on the brain like opioids and other drugs of abuse. They cause changes at the cellular and brain-circuit level, which lead individuals to develop a strong preference for them, via conditioning (Wilcox 2021). Foods in their more natural forms do not. (You'll learn about the particular mechanisms that drive this in chapters 3–5.)

Is It the Food or the Behavior?

Food addiction is defined as "a substance-based addiction to highly palatable foods containing unnaturally high concentrations of refined carbohydrates and fat" (Hoover et al. 2023; Schulte, Avena, and Gearhardt 2015).

The use of "substance" here, as opposed to "behavior," is key. In a behavioral addiction, also known as a process addiction, it's the act of doing something—engaging in a behavior— that primarily reinforces and causes the addiction. Examples of a behavioral addiction include gambling disorder, sex addiction, and internet addiction.

In a substance addiction, the *substance* is the problem. Food addiction is primarily a substance addiction, not a behavioral addiction, because it's not the behavior of eating that's causing the problem, but a particular set of substances that are to blame: namely high-sugar, ultra-processed foods. A substance use disorder results from repeated exposure to a substance that has direct effects on brain chemistry, causing a cascade of neurobiological effects that lead to problems such as addictive behavior. With food addiction, it's primarily the chemical properties of ultra-processed foods that are causing the reinforcement, not the behavior of eating in general.

That said, behavioral addictions have a lot of overlap with substance use disorders, and by extension food addiction. In all three sets of disorders, the reward circuitry is activated, and the pleasure or relief of distress achieved by engaging in the addictive behavior causes a similar kind of associative learning process in the brain. In gambling disorder, the casino lights and smells and noises serve as cues that reinforce the behavior. People with addiction are also inundated with cues related to their substance of choice and susceptible to losing control when exposed to them in a similar manner.

For the majority of people with food addiction, their problem comes from, and is perpetuated by, overexposure to high-sugar ultra-processed foods, not foods in general. Therefore, in most cases, food addiction is a substance addiction. A small subset of people with food addiction binge on any foods, even those with a low addictive potential, like broccoli. People with this problem are sometimes said to have "volume addiction." For these individuals, it may indeed be that it's the behavior of eating, and not the substance itself, that's reinforcing. We'll talk more about volume addiction later in the book, in chapter 8.

The Clinical Perspective

Up until now, we've talked about the colloquial and scientific definitions of addiction. There is also the clinical definition of addiction, aka "substance use disorder," as defined by the Diagnostic and Statistical Manual of Mental Disorders, Fifth Edition (otherwise known as the DSM-5), used ubiquitously by clinicians to diagnose mental health problems. The DSM-5 offers eleven criteria for a substance use disorder, which can be sub-grouped into four key categories: loss of control, time spent, risky problematic use, and physiological symptoms (American Psychiatric Association 2013). These criteria apply to food.

People with food addiction are not in control of their behavior around certain foods (especially high-sugar ultra-processed foods); engage in risky behaviors around them; spend lots of time seeking and eating and recovering from binges (at the expense of their personal and professional lives); and have experienced tolerance and withdrawal from them.

Although we'll go into much more detail about these criteria in chapter 6, and show you how to assess yourself for food addiction, know that there is now extensive evidence, and hundreds of studies in clinical populations, to support claims that food can cause and sustain a syndrome very similar to those seen with alcohol, nicotine, and other substance use disorders (Wilcox 2021; Ifland et al. 2009).

About Obesity

You may have noticed I've used the term "obesity" several times so far, and I will continue using this term and occasionally the terms "overweight" or "normal weight." Just so you know the definitions: a person is considered overweight if they have a body mass index (BMI) of > 25, obese if their BMI is > 30, and normal weight if their BMI is between 18.5-25.

These are medical terms, and many important studies have used the terms to categorize participants so they can draw useful conclusions from their data. That said, it's also important to recognize that the labeling of "obesity" as a disorder or health condition by our medical establishment is of questionable value and validity. Many believe that the cutoffs and categories for normal weight, overweight, and obesity are arbitrary, not based in research, and that BMI is given disproportionate emphasis in evaluations of health. Although it's true that someone whose BMI is > 30 is at statistically higher risk of some health problems than someone with a BMI between 18 and 25, a significant proportion of people with "obesity" are quite healthy. Robert Lustig, endocrinologist and author of *Fat Chance*, said obesity is a "red herring" and explained why he thinks sugar, not body weight, is the primary driver of metabolic syndrome (a precursor of diabetes and heart disease) during his appearance on *Food Junkies* (Lustig 2021). For example, 10-30 percent of people that are "obese" are metabolically healthy (Ojalehto Lindfors et al. 2024), without signs of looming diabetes or cardiovascular disease, and 40 percent of the "normal weight" population have diagnosed metabolic syndrome (Lustig 2021). Similarly, most people with obesity (up to 84 percent) don't struggle with a binge eating disorder (di Giacomo et al. 2022). Designating "obesity" as a medical condition may benefit the drug industry—through blockbuster sales of weight loss drugs—more than the public's health (Katz 2023; Dennis 2021a, 2021b; Lustig 2021; Taubes 2021).

In my opinion, obesity in and of itself is not a problem, and labeling obesity as a disease is misguided. I am absolutely a supporter of body positivity and weight-inclusive care approaches like Health at Every Size. Many people are perfectly happy and healthy and 100 percent functional in larger bodies! Similarly, I believe the terms "overweight" and "normal weight" are problematic and can become a source of oppression, implying a standard to which all people should conform.

However, if someone has obesity plus health conditions that result from the extra weight, or mobility issues or other kinds of functional impair-

> ment, it is important to name the higher body weight as a likely contributor and not sweep it under the rug. Higher body weight also increases risk for medical and behavioral problems. Body weight, for this reason, is still a valid and helpful data point. Therefore, throughout the book I will continue to use the terms "obesity," "overweight," and "normal weight" when reporting research findings, because if I didn't, I would be failing to give you all the information you need to work toward creating this new, rich life for yourself.

The Consequences of Food Addiction

Addiction to high-sugar, ultra-processed food creates numerous problems. You may experience some of them yourself. Is your weight higher than you are comfortable with? Do you struggle with binge eating, mood swings, diagnosed depression or anxiety, diabetes, high cholesterol or triglycerides, or limited physical mobility (arthritis, back pain) made worse by higher than desired body weight? It could be that food addiction is the underlying cause: food addiction increases the risk of weight gain and obesity (LaFata and Gearhardt 2022). Although many people with obesity do not have food addiction, studies show that as many as 20–50 percent do (Meseri and Akanalci 2020); this is higher than the general prevalence of food addiction, which is 15–20 percent (LaFata and Gearhardt 2022).

Food addiction is also a causal factor for some eating disorders. Two *DSM-V* defined eating disorders, bulimia nervosa and binge eating disorder, are defined by the presence of significant binge eating, which is compulsively overeating a large amount of food—far more than what most people would eat—within a discrete period of time. For binge eating disorder, you need to experience binge eating at least once a week. If you use compensatory measures, like vomiting or excessive exercise to get rid of unwanted calories, you likely have bulimia nervosa instead (American Psychiatric Association 2013).

Studies show that 55–80 percent of people with binge eating disorder and 48–95 percent of individuals with bulimia nervosa have food addiction (LaFata and Gearhardt 2022; Wiss 2022a). Food addiction is highly prevalent in these disorders and it's likely that food addiction is an underrecognized cause and contributor to both of these disorders.

Depression, anxiety, and attention deficit disorder occur at higher rates in people with food addiction than the general population, as does metabolic syndrome and other health problems (Wilcox 2021).

Although food addiction can fuel obesity and eating disorders, food addiction is not the same as obesity, and it is not the same as binge eating disorder or bulimia. It is its own beast, with its own unique biological underpinnings. We know this to be true for several reasons. For one, food addiction can occur in anyone—whether underweight, overweight, or normal weight, and whether or not an eating disorder is present. In one study, 43 percent of people with food addiction were obese and 21 percent were overweight (Hauck et al. 2017), and in another, 89 percent were overweight or obese, but 11 percent were normal weight (Pedram et al. 2013). Also, a significant number of individuals with food addiction do not have eating disorders; the prevalences of eating disorders in the general population are much lower than that of food addiction—1–3 percent for anorexia or bulimia nervosa (LaFata and Gearhardt 2022) and 1–7 percent for binge eating disorder (di Giacomo et al. 2022) versus 15–20 percent for food addiction. Relatedly, descriptive studies show that many people with food addiction don't binge eat (Gearhardt 2024).

Still Skeptical?

Are you still not sure whether or not to believe that high-sugar, ultra-processed food is addictive? It's totally fine; I was skeptical too, for a while. That's why I spent a couple years digging through the research to write a textbook about it. If it's not obvious, I no longer have any doubts.

But assuming you do, here are a few common reasons people hesitate to buy the concept, followed by counterarguments against them.

- **We have to eat to live, so it's crazy to call food addictive.** I actually agree that calling all food addictive *is* crazy because we have to eat to live. But, we *don't* have to eat overprocessed food to live. And I believe that calling such foods addictive is not crazy at all.

- **High-sugar, ultra-processed foods are not addictive because not all people get addicted to them**. True. Only a subset of people develop an issue with these foods; according to the Yale Food Addiction Scale (YFAS), a commonly used diagnostic tool, as many as 80 percent don't meet criteria at a single point in time (Pursey et al. 2014). Many people can eat these foods with impunity their whole lives, managing the occasional cravings or overeating episodes with just a little bit of extra exercise, mindfulness, or dieting to maintain their health. However, a good proportion of us do develop an issue. That only a subset of people lose control of eating these foods is a weak argument for not labeling high-sugar, ultra-processed foods as addictive. For example, the majority of people who drink alcohol also don't develop an alcohol use disorder—only 20 percent do over a lifetime, and at any one time 10 percent of our population has one (American Psychiatric Association 2024).

- **People with food addiction don't experience withdrawal symptoms like they do from alcohol, nicotine, and other drugs.** Actually, many of us with food addiction *do* experience withdrawal symptoms when we stop. Many of the experts treating and studying food addiction agree. Phil Werdell, founder of SHiFT Recovery by ACORN (which has treated thousands of people with food addiction in residential settings), once noted that people often go through withdrawal for the first three days in his program after they stop eating ultra-processed foods, with resolution by around day 4–5; common symptoms include nausea, headache, sleepiness, vomiting, and irritability (Werdell 2022). Eric Westman, associate professor of medicine at Duke University and obesity medicine expert, sees a similar set of symptoms when people begin his weight loss program, which uses a low carbohydrate food plan (Westman 2021). Nicole Avena, neuroscientist and author of *What to Eat When You're Pregnant*, has observed and defined a characteristic sugar withdrawal syndrome in the laboratory-based animal models of sugar addiction she has developed. Her rats lick more frequently and engage in other characteristic behaviors similar to what is seen during opioid withdrawal when they have their sugar access cut off (Avena 2021). Finally, Erica La Fata (formerly Schulte), clinical psychologist and researcher, has developed and validated a food withdrawal scale, borrowing from the Wisconsin Smoking Withdrawal Scale already used to identify withdrawal in smokers (measuring factors such as irritability, headache, and sleep) (Schulte 2022; Schulte et al. 2018; Parnarouskis et al. 2020). George Koob, director of the National Institute on Alcohol Abuse and Alcoholism (NIAAA), emphasizes that the absence of somatic symptoms in humans during food withdrawal (e.g. heart rate elevations or tremor) does not mean that withdrawal is not occurring; withdrawal can be defined by subjective symptoms, as it is with nicotine use disorder (Koob 2024).

- **Food can't be addictive if we haven't yet identified the exact molecule or molecules that make it so.** As Chris van Tulleken, author of *Ultra-Processed People*, shared on *Food Junkies*, the fact that we don't yet know the particular chemical or set of chemicals that define addictiveness shouldn't matter (Van Tulleken 2023). We become addicted to the foods that light up our reward network, regardless of the individual ingredients, and it is increasingly clear what characteristics are most important (see chapter 2).

All in all, the consensus is clear: some food *is* addictive.

A Solution That Acknowledges the Facts

Some of us figure out how to stop the out-of-control eating, get free of the tyranny of food cravings, and achieve a comfortable weight through dietary changes, weight loss medications, and/or treatment in an eating disorders model of care. An even smaller portion of us are able to maintain these changes over the long term.

When we embrace the truth—that high-sugar, ultra-processed foods have altered our brain chemistry, fueling their own overconsumption—the solution practically writes itself and things become much easier for us. Abstinence—be it from cigarettes, alcohol, or cocaine—is often the easiest path to long-term recovery for most substances, because the craving, obsession, and unwanted behavior are extinguished: they dissipate. Cutting back can work too. Similar solutions will work when we can't control our use of high-sugar, ultra-processed food.

The reason cutting back or quitting works for addiction recovery is explained, in part, by a biological process called *extinction*. Extinction is the mechanism by which our brains unlearn habits. It's basically the reverse of psychological conditioning. The more we avoid linking the environmental or interoceptive cues with the behavior of using and the experience of reward, the less we have craving, obsession, and unwanted behavior. In other words, the less we use, the less the substance-associated cues have the power to capture our attention and trigger maladaptive habitual behavior.

Letting go of drugs and alcohol is no easy task. It's even harder, for many reasons, to let go of problematic foods. Also, it can be hard to identify personal trigger foods—there are more shades of grey with food than drugs or alcohol—as well as to practice abstinence or reduction. But for now, just remember that with food addiction, it's the high-sugar, ultra-processed foods that are most problematic, not foods in general. There will be all sorts of help and structure in part 2 to help you do all of it.

In summary, addiction centers around a core problem: loss of control. Neuroscience research says that high-sugar, ultra-processed foods are addictive, and people relate to them in the same way that others relate to substances of abuse. The addictiveness of these foods causes adverse physical and mental health. In the next chapter, we'll dive more deeply into which foods are problematic and why.

CHAPTER 2

Which Foods Are Problematic?

"Refined carbohydrates plus fat...and calorie dense combinations of sugar and fat really push reward buttons."

—Stephan Guyenet, *Food Junkies Podcast*

What exactly are "high-sugar ultra-processed foods"? More likely than not, it's the food that you tend to overeat most. There are several ways to determine a food's addictiveness, including the speed with which it's absorbed, the degree to which it's processed, its macronutrient and/or salt content, and more, which we'll discuss at length in this chapter. The addictiveness of food could also be placed on a spectrum: At one end are the ultra-processed and high-sugar foods. On the other are eggs, leafy greens, cucumbers, and other foods that we eat in their unprocessed natural forms. "Organic," "low sugar," or "low fat" labels do not mean the food is not addictive.

According to one study that asked people to rate how likely a food was to be associated with addictive symptoms (using the YFAS, a widely utilized, validated scale you'll be hearing much more about), addictive foods include cakes, cookies, desserts, pastries, pizza, candy, chips, ice cream, processed cereals, and sugary drinks (see Table 1). The least problematic foods are the ones that are the least processed: whole grains; unprocessed meats and fish; legumes; nuts; and fresh vegetables and fruit. The authors concluded that highly processed foods with added fat and/or refined carbohydrates (like sugar and white flour) were most likely to be associated with addictive eating, whereas foods in their natural forms were least likely to be addictive.

Table 1: Food Ranked in Addictiveness from Highest to Lowest

(adapted from Schulte, Avena, and Gearhardt 2015)

Food	Processed	Glycemic Load
Pizza	Y	22
Chocolate	Y	14
Chips	Y	12
Cookie	Y	7
Ice Cream	Y	14
French Fries	Y	21
Cheeseburger	Y	17
Soda	Y	16
Cake	Y	24
Cheese	N	0
Bacon	N	0
Rolls (plain)	Y	15
Popcorn (buttered)	Y	26
Breakfast Cereal	Y	22
Steak	N	0
Nuts	N	3
Eggs	N	0
Crackers	Y	11
Salmon	N	0
Banana	N	12
Brown Rice (plain)	N	20
Apple	N	0
Beans	N	7
Carrots	N	2
Cucumber	N	0

Where to draw the line on what is addictive and what isn't with food is not as clear as it is with alcohol and drugs. Your list of problematic foods may be different from mine, and in later chapters, you'll get some guidance about how to discern what foods prime *your* reward system.

Still, there are some general characteristics that increase a food's addictiveness, which you'll learn about in this chapter. I invite you to consider which system resonates for you best and ponder your own list of problematic foods.

Relatedly, although complete abstinence from alcohol and cigarettes is realistic as a recovery plan, the idea of being perfectly abstinent from all high-sugar ultra-processed foods is not realistic for most of us. In chapter 8, you will learn how to account for this reality in developing your food plan. For now, know that once you understand the characteristics of typical problem foods, it'll be easier to understand which foods are driving *your* food addiction and to work toward a solution that will get you well.

What Makes a Food Addictive?

Again, there are several qualities that make foods addictive: the amount of sugar they have, the degree of processing they've been through, their macronutrient and salt content, and how quickly they "hit" our brains.

Sugar

Sugar is unambiguously addictive. Laboratory studies in rodent models confirm that sugar causes the same behaviors and symptoms as those caused by addictive substances like heroin and cocaine. Laboratory rats who have been overexposed to sugar experience sugar withdrawal and will overconsume sugar, ignoring healthier, readily available rat chow and making themselves sick (Wilcox 2021; Avena 2021).

Sugar in its many forms is often added to ultra-processed foods in unnaturally high quantities to make them more palatable and rewarding—a classic play by the food industry. Some common forms include table sugar, high fructose corn syrup, fruit juice, fruit juice concentrate, maltodextrin, honey, maple syrup, date syrup, corn dextrin, maple sugar, molasses, monk juice concentrate, brown rice syrup, coconut syrup, tapioca syrup, all-fruit jelly, and agave. The Added Sugar Repository, originally developed by the

Eradicate Childhood Obesity Foundation, lists 262 types of sugar (see the Resources List at http://www.newharbinger.com/54681 for more), many of which are added to our food, and act biochemically on our bodies and brains just like sugar. Go look at the backs of packages and you'll see how many of them have sugar (in one of its forms) on the ingredient list: fourth ingredient or higher can be used as a criteria for "high-sugar" food.

Some of you may question seeing honey or maple syrup on the list. Many people think of honey and maple syrup as unprocessed, natural, and therefore not in the same category as table sugar. But biochemically, in terms of what our brain sees, these are just other forms of concentrated sugar in a low-fiber form, and when added to something in just the right amount, they can end up being just as problematic for our sensitive brains. Honey and maple syrup are thus often added to foods in the factory to make them more rewarding, and therefore more addictive.

But, you might wonder, don't we need some sugar to survive? Yes, of course we need glucose to live, because it's where we get our energy. I'm not saying that all glucose is a problem. Nor does "sugar," in this book, refer to carbohydrates in general. Carbohydrates—especially in their whole-grain forms, like brown rice or quinoa—are often not problematic at all. I am also not referring to fresh fruit when I speak of sugar. Although fruits are rich in glucose and fructose, which are primary components of table sugar, fresh fruit is also full of fiber. Therefore, the intensity of the reward experience is dampened compared to when we consume it as the other forms of sugar listed previously. Sugar also does not mean flour. It does not mean bread or pasta, which are refined carbohydrates—although it's important to mention that flour, bread, and pasta are quite addictively triggering for some individuals. Ultimately, the more unambiguously problematic forms of sugar are ones that are purer and more rapidly absorbed, and will be what I'm referring to when I say "sugar" throughout this book.

Degree of Processing

Another way to assess a food's addictiveness is by the degree to which it is ultra-processed, and the NOVA scale helps us decide where it falls on this spectrum. Since its development in 2009, there have been numerous studies backing the scale's validity and it is now used worldwide for public health research. Research demonstrates that people who eat a higher percentage of ultra-processed food—foods designed to be convenient and hyperpalatable, manufactured with industrial techniques, and containing additives and ingredients not normally found in nature—are more likely to have numerous health problems, including metabolic syndrome, cardiovascular risk, type 2 diabetes, dementia, and breast cancer (Callahan 2023; Gomes Goncalves et al. 2023).

NOVA categorizes foods into four groups:

- Group 1 foods (unprocessed or minimally processed) are foods in their natural forms, without added salt or cooking, such as vegetables, meat, milk, eggs, legumes, nuts, dried fruit, fruit juice, wheat flour, grains, plain steel-cut oats, and shredded wheat.

- Group 2 foods (processed culinary ingredients) are made directly from Group 1 foods through cooking or pressing, like oils and fats, sugar, honey, and salt.

- Group 3 foods (processed food) are industrial products made by adding salt, sugar, or other substances found in Group 2 to Group 1 foods and include cheese, bacon, tuna, and industrial breads made only from wheat flour, water, salt, and yeast.

- Group 4 foods are ones that have been mass produced to increase palatability and convenience, and contain emulsifiers, coloring, or added flavor. They include carbonated soft drinks, sweet or savory packaged snacks; chocolate; candy; ice cream; mass-produced packaged breads and buns (with emulsifiers); margarines and other spreads; cookies; pastries; cakes and cake mixes; breakfast cereals; pre-prepared pies and pasta and pizza dishes; poultry and fish "nuggets" and "sticks"; sausages, burgers, hot dogs, and other reconstituted meat products; and powdered and packaged "instant" soups, noodles, and desserts. (Monteiro et al. 2019)

Compare these categorizations with Table 1 from earlier. Two different avenues of research have come up with very similar results: the more the processing, the more likely food is to be addictive. But keep in mind that while the different approaches produce similar results with a lot of overlap, they are not identical. I want to give you all the facts rather than over-simplify because it will help you develop the personal food plan that works best for you later in chapter 8.

Macronutrient and Salt Content

The addictiveness of a particular food can also be defined by its palatability, which is a product of its macronutrient content and proportions thereof. When I stopped eating high-sugar, ultra-processed foods, the addicted parts of myself started looking for ways to make foods at home that would satisfy my cravings—though these solutions eventually became problematic themselves. I learned to make chocolate chip cookies and a blueberry pie that were entirely date-sweetened and still totally binge-worthy. I learned that with a perfect combination of whole-wheat flour, fruit, butter, and salt, I could make to-die-for biscuits. Plain, homemade whole wheat bread didn't interest me much, but when I added a ton of salted butter, I was off to the races. It was so confusing. Nothing was "ultra-processed" or "high sugar," and all the individual items were "healthy," but their combinations were delectable…in a bad way.

Studies have shown that foods that are hyperpalatable—that taste great and have a higher motivational appeal—fall into one of three categories based on the levels of their component macronutrients. Researchers identified three groupings that were most hyperpalatable:

- high in protein and high in sodium (bacon, hot dog, pizza)
- high in fat and simple sugars (desserts like chocolate, cake, ice cream, brownies)
- high in carbohydrates and sodium (breads, snacks like pretzels and crackers, popcorn, biscuits) (Callahan 2023; Fazzino, Rohde, and Sullivan 2019)

When I learned what the common "hyperpalatable" groupings were, the lightbulb went on. I was addicted to the "fat and simple sugars" and "carbohydrates and sodium" categories! It wasn't as black and white as one macronutrient or another.

I personally resonate with this way of flagging a food's addictiveness because it doesn't limit us to just the ones made in factories. We *can* make food addictive at home, out of "healthy" individual ingredients. Most of the food industry's food is crafted with these ratios in mind too; I was just recreating ultra-processed foods at home.

Faster-Acting Foods

There's a fourth way to determine a food's addictiveness: how quickly it acts on our reward network. Foods that hit fast, within seconds of when we consume them (as if injected), are more addictive than ones that are absorbed slowly and take minutes to hours to change our blood sugar levels (and to stimulate the reward circuitry), like whole foods. That's why many of us with food addiction tend to lose control with ice cream but can still eat fruit moderately, even though both items are full of sugar.

What are the foods that activate our reward system faster? Foods that are ultra-processed, high in carbohydrates, low in fiber or protein, soft, and rapidly absorbed. This is the addictiveness heuristic that Chris van Tulleken emphasized on his aforementioned *Food Junkies* interview. These foods taste good, and they tend to have a higher calorie density (number of calories per gram) (Van Tulleken 2023). Again, we're looking at the typical list of foods: cakes, cookies, sugary soda, sausage, chocolate, bread, and more.

That speed of onset is an important factor is also consistent with the study presented in Table 1. Glycemic index is a value assigned to certain foods that reflects how fast the blood glucose rises after eating it. It's a helpful marker for people with diabetes trying to limit their blood glucose levels, and it, too, is a marker that reflects speed of onset. Refined carbohydrates like white flour have a high glycemic index, and fat, protein, and fiber reduce glycemic index. The infographics developed by UK general practitioner David Unwin (Project 2024; Unwin 2021a; Unwin 2021b) are also very helpful for determining glycemic load.

Which foods are slower to hit and therefore less problematic? Foods in their natural forms, like fruit (as opposed to juice, which is lower in fiber) or steak (as opposed to a burger, which is chopped up) are less addictive (Van Tulleken 2023). Meals with harder textures that require slower consumption cause people to take in less calories compared to meals that are more processed and softer (Callahan 2023).

In the substance-use disorder field, it is well established that a drug's speed of delivery influences its addictiveness: IV drugs, which hit the brain fast, are more addictive than oral forms of the same drug, for example. Nicotine (nicotine patch) or opioids (methadone) in slow-release form are less addictive than their smoked counterparts (cigarettes and heroin). The reason for this is that their dopamine spike occurs more proximally in time to the actual behavior that's being reinforced, so the conditioning process is more robust.

One key moment that tipped Michael Moss into being a believer in food addiction was when he learned how sugar acts more quickly on the brain than many established addictive substances. Cigarettes take ten seconds, and pain pills up to twenty minutes, to fully engage the brain. Sugar takes one second (Moss 2021). Using this rationale, sugar and ultra-processed food is not only as addictive as other substances of abuse, but possibly more addictive.

Areas of Controversy

At this point, you've learned a lot of ways to define a food's addictiveness. There are additional factors that may contribute to addictiveness, which I'm going to discuss below, in case you feel like they apply to you in particular.

- **Artificial sweeteners (monk fruit, Truvia, aspartame, etc.):** Some experts think these items also activate the reward system and can keep the addiction alive, in addition to having adverse effects on the gut microbiome, inflammatory markers, and blood sugar. Others—like Nicole Avena, who calls artificial sweeteners the "methadone of sugar"—feel that they may be helpful as a bridge, to help people wean off (Avena 2021; Taubes 2021; Wiss 2021a, 2021b; Goran and Avena 2021; Westman 2021). I'd say follow what feels right for you on this; personally, I avoid them because I don't enjoy the flavor, but the research is too sparse to make a blanket statement about them.

- **Fat:** Decades ago, we were told that fat was bad because it had a high caloric density and caused heart attacks. In the '90s, the food industry pumped out loads of carbohydrate-rich, low-fat foods to accommodate, to which we got hooked, too. Now we are finding out that fat, even saturated fat, has numerous health benefits. Although fat does have a higher calorie density than other macronutrients and may have some risk of causing addiction (Sarkar, Kochhar, and Khan 2019), evidence is sparse and weak, said investigative journalist Nina Teicholz, author of *The Big Fat Surprise*, during her appearance on *Food Junkies* (Teicholz 2023). In a personal communication, Clarissa and Molly of *Food Junkies* note they rarely see pure fat addiction (e.g., eating sticks of butter) in their practice; they *do* have clients that binge on peanut butter, but attribute that to its carbohydrate content. Any fat has the potential to be problematic when combined with carbohydrates (and salt) in certain "hyperpalatable" ratios. As a scientist and pioneer in the academic study of food addiction, Caroline Davis says about ice cream on the *Food Junkies Podcast*: "It's the fat that puts on the weight, but it's the sugar that causes the problem [of eating addictively]" (Davis 2023).

- **Carbohydrates:** Some people believe that carbohydrate content is what makes a food addictive (Unwin 2021a; Unwin 2021b; Westman 2021). As we learned earlier, glycemic load does relate to a food's addictiveness, and sugar and refined carbohydrates are also high-risk for many of us. Also, it's inarguable that the keto and Atkins diets, which are also low-carbohydrate diets, reduce cravings. Some people with food addiction do best when they adopt a low-carbohydrate food plan. However, many people find such food plans too restrictive and can set people up unnecessarily for binge eating in the long run. Some experts feel that villainizing all carbohydrates for all people would be a problematic way to approach the problem, and that high fiber foods like quinoa or fresh fruit (and even less fibrous carbohydrates) should be considered generally safe, until proven otherwise (Dennis 2021a; Wiss 2021a, 2021b).

- **Rarely, the occasional whole food:** Also, some whole or natural foods can end up being problematic for certain individuals with food addiction, often because of their naturally high sugar content. Bananas, dates, and raisins can cause problems for vulnerable individuals.

- **Gluten and dairy:** Some experts think these items also activate the reward system and can keep the addiction alive, in addition to having inflammatory markers and adverse effects on the gut microbiome. My opinion is that there is currently inadequate information to support or refute their addictiveness. However, if you'd like to learn more about dairy, gluten, and the other areas of controversy, check out the list of content-specific *Food Junkies* episodes at http://www.newharbinger.com/54681.

Ultimately, here are the foods experts most consistently deem higher risk when it comes to food addiction:

- Sugar, honey, maple syrup, agave, foods produced with added sugar

- Ultra-processed foods, especially anything made in a factory

- Foods made at home that you crave and overeat and/or that have the macronutrient ratios seen in hyperpalatable foods

- Foods on the top of the "addictiveness" list (hamburgers, fries, pizza, cookies, cake, ice cream, chips, and the like), which can include foods with a high glycemic index

- Soft, low fiber, "fast acting" foods—many people with food addiction let go of flour of all kinds, especially white flour but also whole wheat and other flours, including gluten-free brands.

Exercise: **Reflecting on What You've Learned**

Now I invite you to do a brief journaling exercise. Spend five minutes writing on these questions. What have you learned in this chapter? Do you have any immediate thoughts about which high-sugar, ultra-processed, hyperpalatable, fast-acting foods might be most problematic for you? Keep these personal trigger foods in mind as we move into chapters 3–5, where you will learn more about the process by which addictive foods work on the brain and body to cause addiction and its cornerstone symptom—loss of control.

Highly Rewarding Foods

In conclusion, research shows that there are several ways to define a food's addictiveness potential and that some foods are generally more addictive than others. Although I've been calling the addictive foods "high-sugar, ultra-processed food," I'll be switching from here on out to the term "highly rewarding food." Ultimately, I prefer this term because it's more inclusive and it more accurately reflects the journeys we take. (Again, you'll soon be figuring out what your addictive foods are, and they may not be the same as someone else's.) It also reflects the truth that there is still ongoing ambiguity in the field about exactly what makes food addictive versus not.

CHAPTER 3

The Neurobiology of Overeating: The Homeostatic and Hedonic Systems

"The more you feed a sweet tooth, the more likely it is to grow into a sweet fang."

—David Katz, *Food Junkies Podcast*

Have you ever heard that the key to weight loss is to "eat less and move more"? Have you ever questioned why this seemingly straightforward approach often falls short? While it's accurate that an excess of calorie consumption drives weight gain, the flaw in this as a strategy for weight loss, according to researcher and author of *The Hungry Brain* Stephan Guyenet, lies in its erroneous assumption "that calorie intake and energy expenditure is under voluntary control" (Guyenet 2022a). The idea that we can lose weight by reducing our calories is valid, but a calorie reduction model for weight loss is not complete; it fails to consider the brain chemistry.

Motivation, decision making, and behavior all start in the brain. Our motivation to eat and our decisions to do so often occur unconsciously and are hardwired, especially when it comes to foods that have been designed to hook us. This is why it can be so hard to change our eating habits—our brain biology resists it.

Our inclination and urge to consume food are regulated by biological processes that unfold in various bodily organs and tissues, including the brain, gut, pancreas, adipose (fat) tissue, and the parasympathetic and sympathetic nervous system. The communication within and between these organs and tissues involves a network of hormones, neural signals, and other chemicals, including insulin, leptin, ghrelin, dopamine, endogenous opioids, noradrenaline, glutamate, glucose, and triglycerides (Wilcox 2021; Becetti et al. 2023). The ultimate determinations regarding what, how much, and whether to eat, as well as the associated behavioral patterns, are inherently biological and highly complex.

There are three primary systems with hubs in the brain that regulate our food intake: the homeostatic system, the hedonic system, and the stress response system. In this chapter, you'll learn more about the inner workings of the homeostatic and hedonic systems and how overexposure to highly rewarding food alters the functioning of these systems in ways that make you feel addicted and out of control. In the next chapters, you'll find out how highly rewarding food negatively impacts the stress response system (chapter 4), as well as our impulse control and decision making (chapter 5), with similar problematic effects. Then in part 2, you'll find out how to rewire it all back, and when you get there, you'll be armed with the key knowledge these chapters will provide. At the website for this book, http://www.newharbinger.com/54681, you'll find bonus tables and other content that can help you further digest some of the concepts in the next three chapters. Let's begin!

Homeostatic System: We Eat for Nutrition

Before the food addiction concept became popular a few decades ago, researchers and scientists believed that how much, what, and when we ate was mostly determined by activity in our homeostatic system.

The *homeostatic system* is the network of tissues and chemical messages in our bodies that orchestrate many essential physiological processes, including blood pressure, body temperature, blood glucose levels, and electrolytes. This system's primary task is to maintain homeostasis, or stability and equilibrium in our body: keeping things not too high, not too low, but just right. To do its job, the components of this system need to have information about the state of the body, and use mechanisms such as appetite or fullness to nudge it back into balance when needed (Wilcox 2021; Guyenet 2022a).

The homeostatic system, which includes the brain, regulates our eating behavior. One of the homeostatic system's primary objectives is to maintain the body at a specific *set point*. The *set point* is a set fat-mass range, or body weight range (Garvey 2022; Guyenet 2022a) within which the body tries to keep itself. *Homeostatic eating* refers to eating behaviors that we engage in for the purpose of keeping us near that set point. Appetite and satiety (fullness) signals are generated by the homeostatic system. At any moment, it has a read on recent calorie intake or deprivation and knows the energy state of our bodies. If we are deficient in calories, it increases our motivation and drive to eat. If we are overfed, it signals fullness, initially resisting weight gain, and decreases our intake (Wilcox 2021; Guyenet 2022a).

Maintaining homeostasis in regards to food intake depends on communications between the brain (hypothalamus, cortex), gut, pancreas, vagus nerve, and adipose tissue. Neurohormones (such as insulin, ghrelin, and leptin) and nutrient molecules (such as glucose and triglycerides); gut stretch and nutrient receptors; and adipose tissue communicate the energy state of the organism to higher brain centers, triggering satiety or hunger and thereby stimulating or inhibiting homeostatic eating behavior. The sympathetic and parasympathetic nervous systems (of which the vagus nerve is part) also send regulatory signals between the gut and brain about current nutritional status to affect behavior (Wilcox 2021; Guyenet 2022a; Becetti et al. 2023).

Most research into the neurobiology of overeating originally focused on the homeostatic system. In a healthy homeostatic system, insulin (released by the pancreas in response to food intake) and leptin (released by adipose tissue) act as appetite-suppressing neurohormones that signal fullness or satiety, while ghrelin (produced by the stomach) signals hunger to the brain and stimulates appetite.

It is now established that disruptions within this system—for instance, when the release of these hormones or the body's sensitivity to them is altered—play a crucial role in promoting weight gain and resisting weight-loss efforts. As weight increases and eating patterns become dysregulated, so does this system, making it even harder to lose weight.

For example, when people gain weight, their tissues become more and more resistant to the effects of insulin and leptin (Wilcox 2021; Tarman 2019). Studies show that the blood-brain barrier becomes impervious to insulin, too, in people with obesity (Gray, Meijer, and Barrett 2014). As a result, messages that the body is in a repleted energy state never get to the parts of the brain that regulate appetite, and the person continues to feel hungry, and want to eat.

Hedonic System: We Eat for Pleasure

We don't just eat for nutritional reasons or to maintain energy homeostasis. We eat because it tastes good and gives us joy, regardless of whether we are hungry or full. The hedonic system orchestrates what we do to achieve pleasure. Therefore, it is also a major player in the overeating and food addiction problem.

The hedonic system resides primarily in the brain but receives input from peripheral sensory organs, including taste receptors in the tongue, and carbohydrate and fat receptors in the gut (Peuhkuri, Sihvola, and Korpela 2011; Yang 2022; de Araujo et al. 2012; Guyenet 2022a). The hedonic system also receives input from the emotional centers of the brain (which is how our mood influences our inclination to eat) and is affected by blood glucose levels. Its primary messengers are neurotransmitters such as dopamine, endogenous opioids, glutamate, and others. Our inclination to eat for hedonic reasons is influenced by our environment (including sensory cues and places that remind us of past pleasurable eating experiences), as well as the types of food we have eaten in the past and how they have made us feel (Wilcox 2021; Becetti et al. 2023).

The hedonic system motivates us to select foods based on their perceived tastiness, often favoring options that are rich in energy and high in calories. In the past, having a robust hedonic drive to eat was evolutionarily advantageous when food scarcity was a constant threat, encouraging feasting on high-calorie, energy-dense foods when available, to stock up. However, in the contemporary era, dominated by ultra-processed foods that are meticulously crafted to captivate the hedonic system in ways not found in the natural environment, this hedonic component is problematic (Wilcox 2021).

The hedonic system operates through the same neurochemical machinery as other substances that give us pleasure, such as alcohol, nicotine, and illicit drugs. This machinery is often referred to as the *reward network*, or the mesolimbic dopamine system, which resides mostly in the striatum, prefrontal cortex, and midbrain. The neural signatures of hedonic overeating are strikingly similar to what we see with substance addiction, with parallel alterations in neurotransmitter function and operation of the reward, motivational, and decision making networks of the brain (Wilcox 2021).

Highly Rewarding Food Tips Both Systems Out of Balance

You might recall from chapter 1 the 2019 study that demonstrated that a diet heavy in ultra-processed food leads people to consume 500 calories more per day (Hall et al. 2019; Callahan 2023). It provides indisputable evidence that these particular foods drive their own overuse.

How do highly rewarding foods exert such a potent influence on our intake even before weight gain has occurred? For one, they affect signaling within the homeostatic system. Because they're energy-dense, with more calories per gram than natural foods (as we discussed in chapter 2), our stomachs don't stretch as much when we eat them as it does with less dense food (Van Tulleken 2023). Also, diets high in fat and carbohydrates make our stomachs less sensitive to distention, so the vagus nerve doesn't signal back to the brain that we've just eaten (Loper et al. 2021). When the vagus nerve fails to fire, our brains don't get the message that we should feel full despite having eaten an adequate number of calories.

Highly rewarding food also tips the hedonic system out of balance, which will be the focus of the rest of this chapter—since food addiction in particular is driven more by disruptions in the hedonic system than the homeostatic system.

How Highly Rewarding Food Affects the Hedonic System

Kent Berridge, a groundbreaking addiction researcher, conceptualized addiction as having two components. The first is *liking*, which is what we feel when we consume something that makes us happy, high, or euphoric (Morales and Berridge 2020). Liking is what we experience when we enjoy a cookie with our friends or eat a big mac and cheese dinner at the end of a frenetic day.

Wanting is the second element of addiction. Wanting manifests as a compelling drive to obtain and consume a drug or highly pleasurable food. Wanting is at the root of craving and desire. An excess of wanting is what causes someone with a substance use disorder or food addiction to lose control and to use to excess.

Liking is important for planting the seed of addiction, because it's required for the associative learning and conditioning necessary for cravings and habit formation to develop, but liking does not always lead to wanting. For liking to lead to wanting, conditioning needs to occur.

Neurobiology of Reward: Liking

What are the neurochemical signatures of pleasure and joy? Serotonin, endocannabinoids, oxytocin, and endogenous opioids are the main liking chemicals. In his appearance on *Food Junkies*, psychiatrist and coauthor of *The Molecule of More* Daniel Leiberman dubbed these the "here-and-now" molecules because they communicate pleasure (Lieberman 2022). True enough, there's a plethora of data to back the importance of endogenous opioids as the neurotransmitters of pleasure. Study after study show that blocking their release reduces the subjective experience of pleasure (Wilcox 2021).

Dopamine is also released in the brain when rewarding substances are consumed, which initially lead researchers to believe it was the "feel-good" neurotransmitter, like endogenous opioids. However, research over the last several decades indicates its effect on conditioning and wanting may more important (Wilcox 2021).

Ultimately, the reward network responds the same way to ultra-processed foods as it does to other addictive substances: when we consume anything that makes us feel good—be it cocaine, nicotine, or highly rewarding food—the neurotransmitters, endogenous opioids, and dopamine are released in these same brain areas. Functional MRI studies also show that consuming rewards (be it drugs or food) increases activity throughout the reward network—and the greater the activation, the higher the perceived pleasure. People with obesity, food addiction, and binge eating disorder have more activation in these areas (striatum, midbrain, prefrontal cortex) when they consume highly rewarding food (like milkshakes) than people without. And studies show more robust reward network activation to highly palatable food also predicts later weight gain (Wilcox 2021).

Conditioning: How Wanting Takes Hold

Organisms learn from past experience what makes them feel good (positive reinforcement) or what helps them get rid of negative feelings (negative reinforcement). This learning occurs due to a biological process called conditioning. Associative learning causes us to develop a preference for one rewarding substance or experience over another. It also makes us sensitive to substance-related cues in the environment, which is a major reason why these foods seem to take control of our eating habits.

Dopamine is one of the key chemical drivers of conditioned learning. Both substances of abuse and highly rewarding foods cause robust dopamine surges in the reward network of the brain. "Foods rich in fat and sugar can increase dopamine in the striatum as much as 200 percent above normal levels—a similar bump to what's observed with nicotine and alcohol," journalist Yang claims, citing existing research (Yang 2022). The greater the dopamine surge, the more robust the conditioning, and the more powerful influencers of behavior the substance's associated cues will become.

How does highly rewarding food cause a dopamine surge in our reward system, and specifically in our striatum? First, fats and carbohydrates bind to receptors in the gut and taste receptors on the tongue, which directly or indirectly trigger release of dopamine in the reward network (Wilcox 2021; de Araujo et al. 2012; Guyenet 2022a). Second, blood sugar surges can be directly sensed by brain neurons (Reichenbach et al. 2022) and trigger dopamine release in the striatum, too. And again, with dopamine release in the reward network comes learning.

The other neurotransmitter that is required for conditioned learning is *glutamate*, acting via NMDA receptors (Blackwell et al. 2019; Wilcox 2021). Long-term potentiation (LTP) is a chemical process at the neuronal level that allows our brain to learn and change in response to our environments. It explains what psychologist Donald Hebb observed back in the late 1940s, that "neurons that fire together wire together": the more often two neurons are activated at the same time, the stronger their connection becomes (Hebb 1949; Löwel and Singer 1992; Wilcox 2021).

For LTP to occur in the striatum, dopamine and glutamate must *both* be released into the *synapse*, or the space between two neurons, at the same time (Blackwell et al. 2019; Wilcox 2021; Sketriene et al. 2022). After LTP has occurred, it increases the chance that when an upstream neuron is activated, or fires, the downstream neuron will fire too (Wilcox 2021).

As a result of LTP, cue-induced craving takes hold. For example, if one neuron fires upon smelling the scent of cookies baking (a cue) and the other fires upon the act of eating the cookies, the two neurons wire, and the likelihood that a person will try to find cookies and eat them when they smell cookies baking in the future increases, as does their willingness to expend energy to do so (Wilcox 2021).

How quickly does conditioned learning to highly rewarding foods occur? Rapidly. In a *Food Junkies Podcast* interview, neuroscientist Amy Reichelt noted that in rats, ultra-processed food exposure via sugar and/or chocolate shake drinks leads to altered habits around food-seeking within a span of 2–4 weeks (Reichelt 2023). She says their behavioral changes (including an enthusiastic, dog-like excitement whenever their lab technician starts to prepare a familiar sugar solution) are also linked to measurable, visualizable alterations in the striatum and prefrontal cortex within that same time frame

Conditioning effects are also persistent. Neuroimaging studies reveal that individuals with addictive behaviors remain hyperreactive to cues for several weeks after abstaining compared to controls, although fortunately this reactivity diminishes over time abstinent (Wilcox 2021).

How Cues Trigger Wanting and Doing

We've heard how dopamine is released when we consume a reward, that it is one of many messengers of pleasure, and that its release is what causes us to learn. It turns out dopamine is also the wanting chemical (which is why Lieberman dubs it "the molecule of more" because it fuels motivation and arousal). As Guyenet puts it, addictive drugs cause "massive dopamine spikes in the brain...which reprioritizes...behaviors. If your highest priority before was going to work and taking care of your family maybe now your highest priority is to [procure and consume more of the drug]" (Guyenet 2022b). After conditioning has occurred and associative learning has taken place, exposure to drug- or food-related cues in our environment causes large surges of dopamine in our striatum, which grabs our attention (in this case, acting via the type-1 dopamine receptors (D1)).

Glutamate is also important for cue-elicited behavioral activation, acting via the AMPA glutamate receptors. The combined release of glutamate and dopamine in key brain regions heightens motivation, arousal, and compulsive habitual behavior to obtain and consume (Wilcox 2021; Vanderschuren, Di Ciano, and Everitt 2005).

Have you ever heard about "drug priming"? This refers to the process by which exposure to just a little bit of an addictive drug from which a person or lab rat had had a long period of abstinence triggers a quick spiral into a binge (in the case of food, just a taste of ice cream or just one cookie). This, too, depends on dopamine acting at the D1 receptor; the bite is acting as a powerful cue that triggers old compulsive behaviors to take over, right where they left off (Wilcox 2021).

Drug and food cues also activate the reward network in people who have been conditioned to them (through overuse), according to hundreds of functional MRI studies in humans. In terms of food, numerous studies have now shown that individuals who are overweight, obese, or struggle with binge eating exhibit heightened craving when exposed to reward cues (such as pictures or smells of cookies, or even small tastes of sweet foods), as well as increased activity in the striatum and prefrontal cortex. Greater reactivity predicts both future weight gain and less success in dieting, studies show. Also, women tend to exhibit greater reactivity than men, aligning with existing literature indicating that there is a higher prevalence of food addiction in women compared to men (Wilcox 2021).

Here we might consider some clients' experiences, and even my own, to understand what it's like after associative learning has occurred.

Every time Julie drove by a drive-thru location, she had the mysterious onset of intense desire to order and consume a favorite fast food. Every time I passed by the grocery store where I'd purchased cookie dough before (and enjoyed it), I'd salivate and experience intense craving. Every time Kelly, who struggled with opioid addiction, returned home after rehab, she would relapse; she was only able to successfully stop using when she moved to a new city in a new state. Jordan was able to stop eating sweets when he got all of them out of his house, but when he went to work and saw that an office mate had brought in a chocolate cake, his cravings surged, and—out of nowhere, it seemed to him—he had snuck three pieces into his office and consumed them furtively. Dee once thought she could just have a taste of a cookie and stop there. But within twenty minutes, she had consumed an entire box.

What are the cues in the above examples? The fast food signs, the grocery store signs, an entire hometown, surprise exposure to a cake at work, and the taste of the cookie are examples of conditioned cues which, for these struggling individuals, have grown to have undue power to influence their behavior.

In sum, highly rewarding foods rewire our brains in such a way (through conditioning) that make us excessively sensitive to their related food cues. Another way they rewire our brains is through effects on the emotional brain, which is the subject of the next chapter.

CHAPTER 4

The Stress Response System

"What comes up must come down; there's no free ride in the brain."

—George Koob, "Food Addiction: A New Substance Use Disorder"

Recall that there are three primary systems with hubs in the brain that regulate our food intake: the homeostatic system, the hedonic system, and the stress-response system. You learned about the first two, the hedonic and homeostatic systems, in chapter 3. There, you also learned how the hedonic system drives reward, and how overexposure to highly rewarding food can rewire it to cause food addiction.

In this chapter, we'll discuss the third system, the stress response system. You'll find out how highly rewarding food can adversely affect this system, too, like drugs of abuse. In the short run, highly rewarding foods can dampen the stress response, alleviate negative emotional states, and relieve withdrawal symptoms. In the long run, however, they wreak havoc on the physiology of your stress response system and your emotions in ways that only make addictive behavior worse.

Stress Response System: We Eat for Comfort

There are several important bodily structures and chemical messengers that regulate our stress response, our emotional resilience, and create our moods.

The hypothalamic-pituitary axis and adrenal glands are the parts of the brain and body that physically prepare us for stress by releasing cortisol. The sympathetic and parasympathetic nervous systems also play an important role. The sympathetic nervous system becomes active during stress, increasing heart rate and dilating the pupils, while the parasympathetic nervous system relaxes us and has the opposite effect. The brain's amygdala and locus coeruleus are also key hubs of the *limbic system*, the brain's hub for processing stressful stimuli and generating distress, negative emotions, and alarm signals. And our prefrontal cortex helps regulate our emotional responses. Noradrenaline is the most well-known stress and anxiety neurotransmitter, but other neurochemicals, like corticotropin-releasing factor (CRF) and endogenous opioids, play an equally important role in regulating our emotional responses to stress and distress and in emotion regulation.

As is true for many addictive substances, we often consume highly rewarding foods because they give us short-term emotional relief, whether we are conscious of this motivation in the moment or not. According to studies in animal models and humans, stress causes us to prefer highly palatable, high-calorie-density foods (Wilcox 2021). Stress, mediated by elevated cortisol levels, also causes unwanted weight gain, especially in women (Kemp et al. 2023). And food is generally comforting and soothing, from childhood onward.

Grandma gives us cookies when we are sad. We get lollipops when we go to the dentist and hot chocolate on a cold day. As teens and adults, we go get ice cream with friends when we go through a hard breakup. Sugary foods become our go-to when we are feeling down. This is entrenched in our society; the terms "comfort eating" and "emotional eating" are culturally pervasive.

Highly rewarding foods give us emotional relief via a variety of biological mechanisms. For one, bingeing on fat- and carbohydrate-rich foods can release endogenous opioids in our brain (Wilcox 2021). Case in point: Clarissa of *Food Junkies* had a client with opioid use disorder who would binge on bread and butter every time she went through opioid withdrawal. Her client would use this high-fat, high-carbohydrate combination as a salve for her opioid problem. Highly palatable food also dampens our brains' reactivity to stressful stimuli (Wilcox 2021; Koob 2024), reduces activation of the sympathetic nervous system, increases activation of the parasympathetic nervous system (Wilcox 2021; Koob 2024; Lewis-Marlow 2023), and increases tryptophan levels—the precursor of serotonin, a feel-good neurotransmitter (Markus et al. 1998).

Unfortunately, if we regularly use food for its calming effect or to regulate our emotions, it can come with some serious drawbacks.

Tolerance and Withdrawal

Neuroadaptations from repeated use of alcohol, nicotine, and illicit drugs lead to two key physiological consequences called *tolerance* and *withdrawal*, which are characteristic of all addictions (Wilcox 2021). *Tolerance* means that over time, we need more and more of the substance to attain the same desired emotional effect, whether we're seeking reward or relief.

With *withdrawal*, if we suddenly stop using an addictive substance we've been using regularly, we experience symptoms like irritability, anxiety, body pain, and insomnia, as well as high cravings to return to use.

The phenomena of tolerance and withdrawal are often referred to as the *opponent process*. NIAA director George Koob, who has spent his career studying this, also dubs it "the dark side of addiction" (Koob 2024). Initially, he explains, when we use a substance, we feel good (process A). Then when the substance leaves our system, we feel bad (process B). Over time, the B process gets bigger. In fact, it gets so large it subtracts out the A process. Koob admits, in his research, he is "obsessed with the B process," or tolerance and withdrawal. During withdrawal from any addictive substance, we feel increased dysphoria, alexithymia, anxiety, disease, and uncomfortable in our skin—a state of hypersensitivity to the negative that Koob dubs "hyperkatifeia." Over time, and as we progress in our addictions, our motivation to use shifts from reward to relief, due to our need to "self-medicate the hyperkatifeia" (Koob 2024). The longer and more intensely we use, the worse tolerance and withdrawal get. The imbalance builds to a point where we must use the substance to feel normal. When someone has gotten to this point in their addiction, using their substance of choice relieves the symptoms—but it's ultimately self-defeating because it continues to reinforce the problem.

Anna Lembke, psychiatrist and author of *Dopamine Nation*, describes the opponent process this way: if we lean too far into pleasure, our body produces pain because it wants to be in homeostasis. To illustrate this, she uses a gremlin on a seesaw metaphor. When we eat a cookie, it gives us pleasure, then gremlins in our brain hop on the other side to restore homeostasis; but then when you stop eating the cookies, the gremlins are all gathered on the other side of the seesaw, making you feel worse than you did at the start (Lembke 2021a, 2021b).

One of the key neurobiological signatures of tolerance is lower dopamine sensitivity in the brain due to changes in dopamine receptor profiles (Wilcox 2021; Tarman 2024). The more we flood our brains by overuse, the more the dopamine receptors downregulate—this time, the type-2 dopamine (D2) receptors in the striatum.

The biochemistry of withdrawal from substances of abuse is very well mapped out. Interestingly, it looks very similar to our biological response to stress. In both cases, the brain responds by releasing higher levels of CRF, glucocorticoids, noradrenaline, and lower endogenous opioids, causing us to experience anxiety, irritability, depressed mood, and discomfort. Experiments in laboratory rats and human samples show that overuse of highly rewarding foods will leave the same biological footprints that other addictive drugs do, including low D2 receptor levels in the striatum and greater neurobiological stress responses during withdrawal (Wilcox 2021; Koob 2024; Koob 2022).

Clinically, the symptoms are eerily similar for both tolerance and withdrawal, too, when substance-use disorders and highly rewarding food overuse syndromes are compared in both animal and human models. Tolerance manifests in people with food addiction as reduced pleasure over time, and increased meal sizes and frequencies. Withdrawal from food confers a very similar set of symptoms as withdrawal from cocaine, opioids, and nicotine, numerous studies show (Schulte 2022; Schulte et al. 2018; Parnarouskis et al. 2020; Dennis 2021b; Wilcox 2021; Avena 2021).

No wonder the urge to return to the substance is so strong, especially in the early days of stopping; we want to make it all better. People with more severe withdrawal symptoms are less successful with changing their diets to lose weight (Schulte 2022), highlighting the clinical significance of the withdrawal effects in particular. Interestingly, stress-induced eating of palatable food can be blocked with CRF antagonists and with opioid agonists in laboratory-based animal models (Wilcox 2021; Koob 2024).

To add fuel to the fire, withdrawal and stress will also enhance reward-based conditioning processes further, studies show (Stelly et al. 2020; Wilcox 2021). And withdrawal, stress, and negative emotional states also reduce impulse control via numerous mechanisms, including noradrenaline and stress hormone excess.

Negative Reinforcement Learning

In addition to tolerance and withdrawal, another neurobiologically based process called *negative reinforcement* can fuel addictions. Negative reinforcement is the process by which we learn to lean toward behaviors that we know will relieve physical or psychological discomfort. Negative reinforcement learning, therefore, is *not* learning to avoid punishment; a common misconception. Rather it refers to the process where the removal of an aversive stimulus (like negative emotional states) through a behavior (like eating cookies) leads to a higher likelihood of repeating the behavior (Koob 2024), in a similar manner to what was discussed in chapter 3.

If we overuse food for comfort or we use it to self-medicate our hyperkatifeia, it induces conditioning through negative reinforcement learning, the same as if we use it for reward. It's another way that using substances to feel better sets us up for an out-of-control, vicious cycle, inadvertently undermining our best intentions for ourselves.

The neurobiology of negative reinforcement learning overlaps with that of positive reinforcement or reward-based learning, although it might involve additional mechanisms, mediated by opioid and dynorphin receptors in the amygdala (Walker 2012). Behavior learned through negative reinforcement becomes compulsive and habitual, especially when the particular pain or discomfort is re-experienced. Once negative reinforcement has taken hold, intrinsic mood states such as stress, anxiety, and depression now have the power to trigger our addictive drug or food seeking, just like drug- or food-associated stimuli do (Wilcox 2021). In this way, negative cues can be just as salient as the reward cues you learned about in the previous chapter.

Mood and Anxiety Disorders

As is seen with other substance use disorders, food addiction, obesity, and binge eating disorders often come hand-in-hand with depression, other mood disorders, anxiety disorders (including panic disorder and agoraphobia), and chronic stress (Wilcox 2021). Based on the insights gained from this chapter so far, you're probably not too surprised to hear this since stress and negative emotions often drive comfort eating, which can initiate and perpetuate a food addiction problem. Addictive eating, in turn, makes anxiety and depressive symptoms worse since withdrawal exacerbates negative emotional states (Wilcox 2021).

Neuroimaging research has found that people with mood and anxiety disorders and people with substance use disorders share neural circuitry changes. One of the more consistent overlapping findings between these populations is reduced connectivity between the amygdala (which is part of the limbic system and a generator of emotions) and the prefrontal cortex (which regulates our impulses and emotional responses) (Wilcox, Pommy, and Adinoff 2016). Both sets of disorders are marked by trouble regulating one's emotional responses to stimuli; whereas people with depression and anxiety disorders manifest these brain changes in irritability, isolation, or worry, people with substance use disorders (or food addiction!) go to their drugs of choice for relief. We'll come back to this finding in chapter 11, where you'll learn about skills and solutions that will increase connectivity between these two regions and help with emotion regulation, and therefore help you stay away from highly rewarding food, too.

Trauma and Post-Traumatic Stress Disorder

Food addiction and other addictions are also linked with a history of trauma and a diagnosis of post-traumatic stress disorder (PTSD). Trauma is more prevalent in obese individuals than non-obese individuals, especially in women (Kubzansky et al. 2014). Studies show that early life trauma in particular also increases the likelihood of binge eating, and therefore likely plays an important role in some people's food addiction (Wiss and Brewerton 2020; Dennis 2021a; Wiss 2022b; Hoover et al. 2022; Dennis 2021b).

Adverse childhood experiences (ACEs) can be assessed with a widely utilized self-report scale that assesses for childhood trauma by inquiring about various experiences such as sexual abuse, physical abuse, emotional or physical neglect, and family dysfunction (including frequent conflicts, parental divorce, family members with psychiatric conditions, suicide, or substance abuse issues). All forms of childhood trauma, including adverse experiences such as bullying an unhealthy attachment patterns, can increase the risk of later food addiction or eating disorders (Wiss 2022b).

Adult trauma, and how our bodies respond to it, may affect addiction and food addiction risk, too. A prospective study of trauma-exposed women found that women who developed PTSD had a higher risk of gaining weight compared to those who did not develop PTSD symptoms (Kubzansky et al. 2014).

How Trauma Can Fuel Food Addiction

Trauma can fuel addictive behavior via several biological mechanisms. For one, it creates a psychological and emotional environment rich for negative reinforcement processes to occur—the more we experience psychological discomfort, the more we will try to find ways to experience calm and relief, as we talked about in the previous sections.

Trauma and PTSD also adversely affect our impulse control. Studies show childhood trauma and maltreatment may increase the risk of obesity and binge eating by causing impulse control deficits (Hoover et al. 2022). People with PTSD have reduced recruitment of the prefrontal cortex during performance of cognitive tasks compared to controls (Wilcox 2021). High levels of noradrenaline and stress hormones give us insomnia, decrease our cognitive function, and impair decision making, which can make cravings even harder to resist.

Third, trauma can fuel food addiction by increasing reward sensitivity, inducing conditioned learning, and heightening reward motivations (Stelly et al. 2020; Wilcox 2021; Wiss 2022b). People with a trauma history have larger surges in dopamine in the striatum after taking certain drugs, indicating hypersensitivity of reward system. Individuals with PTSD also have brain changes (higher dopamine transporter levels) reflecting a higher dopamine turnover, or chronically higher dopamine activity (Wilcox 2021).

Finally, loss of sleep, commonly seen with PTSD, also increases reactivity of brain reward networks to food cues (Samakidou et al. 2023; Wilcox 2021; Katsunuma et al. 2017).

Weight Stigma as a Source of Stress and Trauma

People in North America and elsewhere are still pressured by social media and unhelpful sociocultural norms to be thin. Weight bias and problematic body image ideals are a major problem in our culture (Kemp et al. 2023). Clarissa of *Food Junkies* reports that most of her clients report a causal relationship between weight discrimination experiences and symptoms of anxiety and depression. When societal stigma gets internalized as shame and low self-esteem, dysphoria rises—which, as we've seen, is a setup for disaster in someone with food addiction. Shaming and stigmatizing drives people further into their addictions (Van Tulleken 2023).

Studies show that it's not body size but the interaction of body size and cultural norms that causes people in larger bodies to struggle with low self-esteem, shame, and mental health issues. In cultures where larger bodies are more accepted, self-esteem is less affected by body weight (Kemp et al. 2023). As further evidence that it's the culture to blame, studies show that perceived obesity is more predictive of comorbid psychiatric conditions than actual obesity (Perry, Guillory, and Dilks 2021). In women—who experience more internalized stigma and for whom pressure to be thin is generally greater than for men—guilt, shame, and low self-esteem are more closely tied to body image (Kemp et al. 2023). Societal pressure is stronger for them. Together, this body of work shows that it's the cultural factors that are to blame for the depression and anxiety, not the obesity itself.

Stigma and pressures from the mental health and medical communities—from individuals who think they are helping—can be further traumatizing to people in larger bodies. Molly Carmel, therapist and author of *Breaking Up With Sugar,* and Kim Dennis, a psychiatrist specializing in addictions and eating disorder treatment, highlight how diet culture's persistence in medicine stigmatizes people in larger bodies, fueling stress, restrictive eating, and rebound binge eating (Carmel 2021; Dennis 2021b).

Weight bias still exists in the food addiction field, too, with some providers holding onto old beliefs that people in larger bodies are not doing well (Dennis 2021b).

If you feel like you've been traumatized by diet culture, you'll learn all sorts of ways to restore your self-esteem and disentangle yourself from ongoing toxic societal messaging in chapters 7 and 11. This will be an essential and achievable part of your recovery from food addiction.

In chapter 3, you learned how overexposure to highly rewarding food makes you sensitive to food-related use, and in this chapter, you learned how highly rewarding food alters your emotional brain to make you susceptible to emotional cues, too. In this next chapter, you'll learn a third mechanism by which highly rewarding food rewires your brain—namely by affecting your impulse control.

CHAPTER 5

Addiction as a Disorder of Decision Making

"Our behavior is as absurd and incomprehensible with respect to the first drink as that of an individual with a passion, say, for jay-walking. He gets a thrill out of skipping in front of fast-moving vehicles.... [After several accidents, and hospital visits], he tells you he has decided to stop jay-walking for good, but in a few weeks he breaks both legs."

—The *Big Book*, Alcoholics Anonymous

Those of us with an addiction often recognize the madness of this jaywalker who keeps crossing the street—each time expecting different results, against all reason. This is because we also often find ourselves making decisions that in retrospect don't make sense and are not in our best interests...especially when it comes to a substance of choice.

Is the maladaptive decision making in addictive disorders due to a character flaw, low intelligence, lack of motivation, or character weakness? No; it's a problem in the neurobiology of the brain.

Addiction is often conceptualized as a disorder of decision making. Decision making is a complex neurocognitive construct, involving processes such as attention, executive control, planning, assignment of value to immediate versus delayed rewards, impulse control, working memory, and emotion regulation (Sehrig, Odenwald, and Rockstroh 2021; Pastor and Medina 2021; Wilcox 2021). The brain structures involved in decision making (executive control) include the prefrontal cortex, anterior cingulate cortex, and insula, which receive input from and send output to the reward system (striatum) and limbic system (amygdala). Dopamine, norepinephrine, and glutamate are several of the key neurotransmitters that work in concert to establish working memory and impulse control.

People with addictions have an imbalance between circuits that stimulate impulsive reward-seeking and those that regulate or control behavior. In chapter 3, you learned about the inner workings of our reward-seeking brain and how overactivating it can derail you. Here you are going to learn about the neurobiology underlying behavioral control, and how it, too, can malfunction in people with substance use disorders and food addiction.

Antoine Bechara, a groundbreaking addiction researcher, puts it this way: "Drugs can trigger bottom-up, involuntary signals…that modulate, bias, or even hijack the goal-driven cognitive resources that are needed for the normal operation of the reflective system and for exercising the willpower to resist drugs" (Bechara 2005). This is to say our decision making, normally under the control of our prefrontal cortices, gets usurped by reward and motivational circuits in the striatum and midbrain when the reward system is overactivated through "bottom-up" processes (Sehrig, Odenwald, and Rockstroh 2021; Pastor and Medina 2021).

But "top-down" processes are also disrupted by highly rewarding food. Like we saw with the hedonic system and the stress response system, overuse of highly rewarding foods also causes direct damage to the prefrontal cortex and other structures that regulate our decision making and impulse control.

What Maladaptive Decision Making Feels Like

Those of us with addictions are familiar with what it feels like to have loss of control. We make a commitment to stop or cut back on consuming something, and we make a firm resolution to change. We adopt a stance of resistance, and we are sure we will stick with it this time. Then somewhere along the way, our resolve disappears, all but abandoned and forgotten. Our lower-order primitive brains—limbic system and striatum—take the reins, never even asking for sign-off from our more intentional, thoughtful, executive control center. Our "Go Brain" (which Michael Moss also calls a "death-defying emergency brain") overcomes our "Stop Brain" (Moss 2021). We go back to whatever we were trying to stay away from, and soon we are caught right back in the destructive cycle.

Sometimes, drug-seeking behavior can seem to arise out of nowhere, unconsciously, without inner conflict or deliberation of any kind. One second, we are sure we're never going to use again. The next, we are in full-blown relapse. My patient, Graham, experienced such unconscious behavior:

- *Graham's Story*

    In an effort to reduce his late-night eating, Graham moved his fridge to a different location and replaced it with a painting. Afterward, he would repeatedly find himself standing in front of the painting, where the fridge used to be, initially puzzled about why he was there—until he remembered that the fridge used to occupy that space.

Paul Earley, an addiction medicine physician and author of *RecoveryMind Training: A Neuroscientific Approach to Treating Addiction*, explains on *Food Junkies* how our brains can become habituated to engage in substance-seeking behaviors even in the absence of explicit craving (Earley 2021).

Both Paul Earley and Graham are describing what happens when decision making processes take place outside of our conscious awareness. Unconsciously engaging in an addictive behavior is akin to scratching an itch—we do it out of habit, often before we've had the chance to assess the wisdom of it. A workaround such as this for food consumption was probably evolutionarily advantageous when rewards were more scarce and quick action to procure nutrients was a matter of life and death.

Our brains also make maladaptive decisions in more conscious and intentional ways, which can also drive addictive behavior. Consider a scenario where, inspired by reading Vera Tarman's book *Food Junkies*, you decide to let go of sugary foods to rid yourself of the distracting cravings and the cloud of depression that's been hanging over you since you began overeating sweet foods a few years ago. You are hopeful this change might help. You have been told that you may feel withdrawal symptoms or intense cravings, but you know they will be temporary, lasting days, and that within a few weeks, you'll start to experience all the benefits. You stop. You feel some urges, but you are able to resist acting on them: likely you are recruiting your prefrontal cortex, where your cognitive control centers are housed. The first day goes well.

However, the next day, a new set of thoughts infiltrate and replace the old ones. You start to tell yourself that depriving yourself like this is unnecessary. You can't remember why you started down this path in the first place. You tell yourself you won't stick with it in the long run and might as well give up now. Or perhaps you convince yourself that you're not that bad off, you can keep eating sugar. You tell yourself you deserve a treat for all your hard work, and no one will notice if you indulge sneakily. Despite having tried the "just one bite" approach countless times before, you tell yourself that this time will be different because you've been eating more vegetables since reading *Food Junkies* too. What begins as a little craving becomes an idea and a series of justifications, which then evolves into a plan, eventually translating into action. You find yourself carrying out the plan, maybe even consuming eight cookies, all the while observing yourself with growing confusion. In a mere forty-eight hours, you're painfully, uncomfortably full, having overindulged once again. The demoralizing realization sets in. But it's only when the justifications are written down and examined that their irrational nature becomes apparent.

This illustrates the unfortunate reality that our lower-order, primitive, drug-seeking brain can actually trick our executive control brain into doing things that are not in our best interest, duping us into believing that what we are doing *is* in our best interest. They call this kind of rationalization "stinking thinking" in Alcoholics Anonymous (AA). This stinking thinking is also why AA calls addiction "cunning, baffling, and powerful" (Alcoholics Anonymous 2001). It can feel like a genuine state of insanity, and the manifestations of this madness are played out in our brains and bodies.

Once, in a hurry to whip up cookies using all-fruit jelly, I accidentally dropped the jelly jar on the floor, causing its top to shatter. Peering down among the shattered pieces to the jelly, I couldn't see any shiny hard objects, and thought, "Well, I can't spot any glass shards, so I'm probably okay."

With it being the only sweetener at home, I went ahead and made the dough using the jelly.

I took a bite of the dough. On the third bite, I encountered something crunchy—was it glass? It crunched and disappeared. Concerned, I turned to Google and typed in "eating glass dangerous." I read that it could be, and that one woman accidentally ingested a large shard, cut an internal artery, and died. But there were numerous posts that reassured me that small shards likely wouldn't cause harm. The allure of the taste of the dough and the cookies was so strong. These were probably tiny shards, I reasoned, if any more remained. I took a few more bites of the dough, now taking smaller, more cautious bites. When I came upon something crunchy, I pulled the small shard out, or I chewed it into sand. I seemed to still be alive.

I made the cookies and repeated my cautious chewing, occasionally getting the crunch of glass, still relishing the experience despite that. Afterward, when I was finally full, I felt overwhelming shame (and some fear) about what I had done.

When the drug- or food-seeking circuits usurp our decision making and take control, the thoughts that our wonderfully complex and intelligent brain generates can feel like they are coming from the executive, but they are really just the inner rebel talking.

Decision Making Deficits in Addiction and Overeating

What we decide to do in the face of reward-related cues and other triggers depends on our brain chemistry. It is now indisputable that people with substance use disorders have deficits in numerous domains of decision making, and these deficits, if unaddressed, will adversely affect recovery trajectories across a wide variety of substances (Wilcox et al. 2013; Wilcox, Abbott, and Calhoun 2019). Specifically, people with substance use disorders tend to have poorer performance on cognitive tasks, reduced prefrontal cortical brain activation during cognitive tasks, and lower frontal brain volume (grey matter). They also have lower functional connectivity in executive control networks, meaning the parts of the network are not acting in sync, or efficiently (Wilcox et al. 2010; Wilcox 2021).

Dopamine also plays an important role in our cognitive and impulse control. As Lieberman says, it's helpful to conceptually divide dopamine function into two systems: the "dopamine control pathway" and the "dopamine desire pathway" (Lieberman 2022). The dopamine desire pathway we covered in chapter 3. The dopamine control pathway also plays a key role in addictive behavior. It turns out that dopamine dysfunction (reductions in D2 and dopamine transporter levels) causes impulse control and planning deficiencies. Studies show that people with a variety of substance use disorders have these particular changes in dopamine function.

More specifically, research shows that people with obesity and binge eating disorder (populations that have higher rates of food addiction) and people with food addiction display similar brain wiring to those with substance use disorders. For one, they perform more poorly on tasks assessing cognitive flexibility, executive functioning, working memory, impulse control, decision making, attention, and planning in numerous studies (Iceta et al. 2021; Wilcox 2021). They also have reduced frontal grey matter, diminished connectivity in executive control network (Peng-Li et al. 2020), and reduced recruitment of key prefrontal cortical brain regions when they are asked to perform cognitive tasks (Schienle, Unger, and Wabnegger 2020; Wilcox 2021). Studies show that people with obesity also have very similar dopamine receptor deficiency profiles to people with substance use disorder, including low D2 receptor density in the striatum (Wilcox 2021).

Whether it's food, alcohol, or other substances of abuse that are the culprit, any of these aforementioned deficits can cause people to have difficulty staying on task, remembering the reasons that they wanted to quit in the first place, and regulating their impulses. The larger the deficit, the greater the addiction severity.

The Cause

Why do people with addictions, obesity, binge eating, and food addiction have similar cognitive and decision making deficits? Is it because the substance use or the addictive foods cause damage to the brain? Or is it because some preexisting deficiency in impulse control, delayed gratification, or self-regulation predisposes people to develop an addiction?

The science tells us that it's probably a bidirectional relationship. Issues with impulse control, planning, and organizing make someone more vulnerable to developing an addiction in the first place, and make it harder to get a handle on an addiction once it's set in. There is extensive literature in substance use disorders showing that reduced activation in the prefrontal cortex to cognitive tasks, certain genetic markers associated with poor impulse control, low D2 receptor function, and a preference for immediate gratification over long-term gains, for example, predict later development of a substance use disorder (Wilcox 2021). The studies indicate that the same is true for obesity, binge eating disorder, and food addiction.

For example, attention-deficit/hyperactivity disorder (ADHD) is characterized by deficits in executive control, and studies show ADHD is associated with obesity, food addiction, and binge eating, and that the ADHD more often precedes the eating problem (Wilcox 2021; Cortese and Tessari 2017). Studies also show that in people who are already obese, the degree of activation in the dorsolateral prefrontal cortex (an important region for planning and impulse control) predicts the success of weight loss attempts (Wilcox 2021).

It is also well established that excessive consumption of alcohol, stimulants, and nicotine will cause damage to the brain, causing loss in brain volume; reduced recruitment of the prefrontal cortex in the performance of cognitive tasks; dopamine dysfunction in the prefrontal cortex and striatum (including reduced D2 receptor levels in the striatum); and problems with tasks requiring executive control. Similarly, diets high in highly rewarding food can also adversely affect prefrontal cortical function and impair impulse control (Wilcox 2021). Prenatal periods, infancy, childhood, and adolescence are especially sensitive times, and studies show that excess exposure to sugar predicts later cognitive deficits as far in the future as adulthood (Beecher et al. 2021).

Amy Reichelt has studied the ways that ultra-processed foods affect the brain, focusing on the prefrontal cortex and the hippocampus, our brain's memory center. In her laboratory, she has shown that rats switched to diets of pie, cookies, and cake, or diets of high-sugar sucrose water, demonstrate memory, decision making, and impulse control deficits in as little as four to five days. Concurrently, she's found that important modulatory neurons for cognition that reside in the hippocampus and prefrontal cortex, get wiped out in the same timeframe (Reichelt 2023; Reichelt et al. 2015).

Behavioral control and functional decision making processes are essential for habit changing. And people with food addiction who are trying to make changes in their behavior are just the people that need those neurons working more than anyone. But highly rewarding foods deaden those very neurons' functions. It's a vicious cycle.

The Limitations of Our Cognitive Reserves

The more we have to resist cravings for highly rewarding food, the more likely we are to binge, and the more we struggle with complex intellectual tasks (Lieberman 2022). Research has found that the continuous exertion of willpower or self-control is fatiguing (Kahneman 2011). The more you force your brain to work to resist something, the less willingness or ability you have to resist the next challenge that comes along.

Old conditioned brain circuits linger, hiding out in the dark until they find a window of opportunity—a moment of weakness, a lapse in attention—and when they see it, they take their shot. Sometimes when we are craving, we can catch ourselves in time, name it, and see it as just a feeling, then find the strength to sit though the craving until it has passed—perhaps engaging in the technique of "surfing" the urge until it passes, going on a run, or engaging in a pleasurable distracting activity to help it dissolve more quickly. Other times we are less successful.

Our cognitive reserve depletes easily, even in those of us without addictions. In his bestselling book *Thinking, Fast and Slow* (2011), Daniel Kahneman provides ample evidence from human and animal models that we have limits in our capacity to resist, think, and remember. He describes how physical exertion acutely diminishes working memory and attention: even simple tasks, like solving a math problem, become more challenging during a jog, because exercise reduces blood glucose and glucose is needed to keep our control brain online. (Note that this refers to the acute, immediate effects of exercise on attention and cognition, not exercise's long-term, holistic effects, which are quite positive.) He also cites several studies showing that individuals simultaneously confronted with a demanding cognitive task and a temptation are more likely to succumb to the temptation than those not exposed to the demanding task.

None of us has limitless willpower. The more we fight, the smaller reserves we have, and the more vulnerable we are to further triggering, studies show (Lieberman 2022). That's why it's so important that we take good care of ourselves emotionally and avoid cues and triggering situations as much as possible in the early days of our recovery. We never know when our Stop Brains will poop out and our Go Brains will take the lead.

In summary, highly rewarding foods rewire our brains by inhibiting our impulse control and decision making, leading us to prioritize immediate use over delayed rewards through abstention. But the good news is that removing these foods (or reducing our consumption) can restore our brain function over time—perhaps within months of changing our diet, if we go by data from studies in substance use disorders (Wilcox et al. 2013; Volkow et al. 2001; Wilcox 2021; Volkow et al. 2002).

PART 2

Diagnosis, Treatment, and Recovery

CHAPTER 6

Diagnosis and Assessment

"Many of my patients...would spontaneously say to me 'I'm addicted to food' without any prompting whatsoever, and I thought that was interesting...I started asking my patients, 'Do you experience this as an addiction of sort?' and they'd respond, 'Yes, how did you know?' And I got this really dramatic and passionate response from a lot of people and it really kind of enhanced the therapeutic alliance, because they felt like I really understood at a deeper level what they were going through.... It's really important to listen to patients, patients are our best teachers."

—Timothy Brewerton, *Food Junkies Podcast*

Are you thinking you might have a food addiction? In this chapter, you'll get a chance to explore that more deeply. It's important to establish this first because if you aren't addicted, the solution we'll discuss might not apply. Also, remember from chapter 1 that although food addiction is often a factor in obesity, eating disorders, and diabetes, it is NOT present in everyone with these disorders.

First, you'll learn how to determine if your symptoms are severe enough to qualify as food addiction on a validated scale. Then you'll learn how to make sure that your problem is food addiction rather than something else that talks and walks like food addiction but isn't—namely, certain eating disorders. Finally, we'll flag several other common issues that often travel with food addiction, which will help you to refine your personal recovery plan accordingly.

- *Sara's Story*

    Sara always loved to eat. She was physically active in high school and was able to maintain a weight that was comfortable for her. However, in college, her weight started increasing and she began to worry about her health. Over the next decade, she tried everything she could think of, including promotional programs on the radio, Weight Watchers, Jenny Craig, and Nutrisystem. The cravings and obsessions would always win out though, and the more she dieted, the more she binged. She also tried practically every weight-loss medication in the book, which either didn't work or caused side effects. What did work for her, temporarily, were the low-carb diets, like Atkins or keto, but she couldn't seem to stick with any of them for longer than six weeks. Finally, after her BMI hit 35 and she developed knee osteoarthritis, she underwent bariatric surgery in her thirties.

    Sara lost almost one hundred pounds over the first year post-op, although she had complications requiring more surgeries. But after that year, she started eating in the old ways again—more and more Cheetos, crackers, bread, shakes, chocolate, and cake, often called "slider foods" (calorie-dense, fast-acting foods that can bypass the surgical stricture). She regained most of the weight she had lost. Although Sara thinks bariatric surgery was a wonderful tool, it was not a cure, because it wasn't a brain transplant. The concept of food addiction really resonates because she feels her problem is primarily rooted in her brain.

Food Addiction and the DSM

If you approach the mainstream medical field for help with your loss of control around highly rewarding food today, you might be offered referral to a weight loss program, medication, or bariatric surgery. But doctors won't likely tell you how to curb the cravings. It would be very unlikely that they offer you a diagnosis of food addiction. In mainstream medicine, the root cause—that our brains have been rewired by highly rewarding food—is overlooked, in favor of characterizing concerns about loss of control as a matter of willpower or an individual fault, rather than as systemic and due to biology. Therefore, there is no way to officially diagnose someone with food addiction because the term "food addiction" is not in the DSM…yet.

But food addiction definitely exists. Times are changing, thankfully. A growing body of research and increasing acceptance of the construct in academic and some clinical communities will hopefully sway the DSM in the future, since research shows (see chapter 1) that all the criteria for a substance use disorder are met when sugar is the substance. Therefore, even though assessing and diagnosing someone with food addiction is still premature from an "official" perspective, I believe that we will see it as an official diagnosis soon (likely under the name "ultra-processed food use disorder"), and you deserve to learn the criteria that will probably be used to define it without having to wait.

The DSM-V Criteria for a Substance Use Disorder

As I mentioned in chapter 1, the DSM-V, the manual used by addiction professionals and psychiatrists to diagnose an addiction, defines a substance use disorder based on eleven individual criteria (American Psychiatric Association 2013). These criteria can be organized into four categories, as follows.

LOSS OF CONTROL

The DSM-V criteria within this grouping include taking the substance in larger amounts or for longer than originally intended; unsuccessful attempts to quit or cut back; and intense cravings for the substance.

- ### *Eileen's Story*

    Eileen felt like a failure. No matter how many ways she tried, it seemed she was never able to stick with the dietitian-recommended food plan. The evenings were the worst—when she was alone, she couldn't stop thinking about, and ultimately consuming, cookies.

    Loss of control is a hallmark symptom of food addiction. We just can't get a handle on our eating, no matter how hard or long we try.

TIME SPENT

The DSM-V criteria within this grouping include spending an excessive amount of time getting, using, or recovering from the substance at the expense of essential life activities at work, home, school, or recreational activities.

- *Lucy's Story*

    Lucy was trying to change her eating, but she couldn't stick with it. Over the last year, she had skipped three of her friends' weddings—usually cancelling at the last minute—because she felt too ashamed of her recent weight gain, and feared people would judge her for her "weak will." She also cancelled countless internet dates due to body shame, and called in sick to work ten times for food hangovers.

Those of us who struggle with food addiction often isolate ourselves. We also prefer to eat in secret. We have lower quality of life scores and devote much of our days to either eating high quantities of highly rewarding food, or suffering from food hangovers, which often occur after a large binge.

RISKY AND PROBLEMATIC USE

The DSM-V criteria within this grouping include persistent use despite negative consequences in personal relationships, physical health, or psychological health, and even in the face of harm.

- *Jen's Story*

    Jen had always had a predilection for sweets and ate them frequently. She ended up putting on a significant amount of weight by her forties. She had to sleep sitting up because she had intractable acid reflux, causing her to sleep poorly and feel tired during the day. She also had knee osteoarthritis and rarely left the house because of it. The surgeons were unable to help her with either problem; her weight prevented her from being a surgical candidate.

Highly rewarding foods wreak havoc on our bodies and minds. Food addiction can cause excess weight, medical problems, physical limitations, psychological struggles, and stigmatization by society. Highly rewarding food, with or without obesity, also increases the risk for a plethora of conditions including depression, brain fog, anxiety, fatigue, and insomnia, to name just a few. Common risky behaviors include binge eating while driving and eating food out of garbage cans.

PHYSIOLOGICAL

The DSM-V criteria within this grouping include increased tolerance of the substance—needing more and more to achieve the same effect—and the development of withdrawal symptoms when the substance is stopped.

- *My Story*

    Every time I stopped eating sugar or vowed to stop binge eating, I'd experience several days of a withdrawal syndrome including irritability, poor sleep, brain fog, nausea, and headache. The cravings were intense too—not unlike nicotine withdrawal, with which I was also very familiar as an ex-smoker who had quit many times.

Many of us with food addiction experience withdrawal symptoms when we stop. They can get so severe and uncomfortable that they undermine our attempts to change, flipping us into relapse after only a few days. Again, research indicates that food withdrawal in humans does exist, mirroring the time, course, and to some degree the symptomatology of withdrawal from other substances to which we can "get addicted," particularly nicotine.

Some of us with food addiction also experience tolerance. We find ourselves needing increased portion sizes over time to get the same feeling of satisfaction. Tolerance can be low when one relapses after a period of recovery from food addiction, but just as with other substances, it builds and builds over time back to where it was originally.

Now that we've established the ways addiction is characterized in the DSM-V—and you've had a chance to consider whether any of these criteria resonate with your experience—we'll turn to presenting you with a measure that's been developed using these criteria in relation to ultra-processed food.

Yale Food Addiction Scale

The Yale Food Addiction Scale (YFAS) is currently the most widely used assessment tool for food addiction. It is a self-report scale and was derived from the DSM criteria used to define a substance use disorder (Gearhardt, Corbin, and Brownell 2016).

Other diagnostic tools include the CRAVE and UNCOPE, and researchers have developed a clinician-administered scale (Schulte 2022; Gearhardt 2024), but for simplicity we will focus on the YFAS, since it's directly derived from the DSM-V criteria for substance use disorder and is widely used and validated. In this book, for reasons of space, I've decided to provide the questions from a shortened version, the mYFAS, which is almost as accurate as the full YFAS.

Modified Yale Food Addiction Scale Version 2.0

This survey asks about your eating habits in the past year. People sometimes have difficulty controlling how much they eat of certain foods such as:

- Sweets like ice cream, chocolate, doughnuts, cookies, cake, and candy
- Starches like white bread, rolls, pasta, and rice
- Salty snacks like chips, pretzels, and crackers
- Fatty foods like steak, bacon, hamburgers, cheeseburgers, pizza, and French fries
- Sugary drinks like soda pop, lemonade, sports drinks, and energy drinks

When the following questions ask about "CERTAIN FOODS," please think of ANY foods or beverages similar to those listed in the food or beverage groups above, or ANY OTHER foods you have had difficulty with IN THE PAST TWELVE MONTHS.

For each of the thirteen statements below, choose the answer from the below eight options and write your score in the blank.

Never (0)

Less than monthly (1)

Once a month (2)

2–3 times a month (3)

Once a week (4)

2–3 times a week (5)

4–6 times a week (6)

Every day (7)

1. I ate to the point where I felt physically ill. _____

2. I spent a lot of time feeling sluggish or tired from overeating. _____

3. I avoided work, school, or social activities because I was afraid I would overeat there. _____

4. If I had emotional problems because I hadn't eaten certain foods, I would eat those foods to feel better. _____

5. My eating behavior caused me a lot of distress. _____

6. I had significant problems in my life because of food and eating. These may have been problems with my daily routine, work, school, friends, family, or health. _____

7. My overeating got in the way of me taking care of my family or doing household chores. _____

8. I kept eating in the same way even though my eating caused emotional problems. _____

9. Eating the same amount of food did not give me as much enjoyment as it used to. _____

10. I had such strong urges to eat certain foods that I couldn't think of anything else. _____

11. I tried and failed to cut down on or stop eating certain foods. _____

12. I was so distracted by eating that I could have been hurt (e.g., when driving a car, crossing the street, operating machinery). _____

13. My friends or family were worried about how much I overate. _____

SCORING

Step 1. Answer these two questions yes or no: Was item #5 greater than five? Was item #6 greater than five? If you answered no to both these questions, then food addiction is not present.

If at least one is a 1, then keep going.

Step 2. Now answer yes or no for each of the following questions:

Was your score on #1 4 or more?

Was your score on #2 5 or more?

Was your score on #3 2 or more?

Was your score on #4 4 or more?

Was your score on #7 2 or more?

Was your score on #8 4 or more?

Was your score on #9 5 or more?

Was your score on #10 4 or more?

Was your score on #11 5 or more?

Was your score on #12 2 or more?

Was your score on #13 2 or more?

How many yes answers do you have from the above list? _____
(Please exclude the items mentioned in step 1.)

No Food Addiction = 1 or fewer symptoms

Mild Food Addiction = 2 or 3 symptoms

Moderate Food Addiction = 4 or 5 symptoms

Severe Food Addiction = 6 or more symptoms

(Flint et al. 2014; Schulte and Gearhardt 2017)

False Positives on the YFAS

If you score positive on the YFAS, does that mean you have food addiction for sure? The answer is no! The YFAS can give "false positives." This means that other problems can increase the score on the YFAS even if true food addiction is not present—specifically, eating disorders.

An untreated eating disorder with recent excessive dieting and caloric restriction can look symptomatically just like food addiction, if you only go by the DSM diagnostic criteria (Wiss 2022a). This is why it's important for you to stop and consider whether you might have an eating disorder that is masquerading as a food addiction as the root cause of your problem. It's also possible that you might have both (recall from chapter 1 that comorbidity is high), all of which will affect your recovery planning.

First, I will remind you of the definitions (chapter 1), so you know what I am talking about when I refer to eating disorders. *Binge eating disorder* is associated with recurrent episodes of binge eating occurring at least once a week for three months, where people often feel a lack of control over their eating during the episode but do not engage in compensatory measures to prevent weight gain, such as purging (aka vomiting), laxative use, or excessive exercise. *Bulimia nervosa* also involves binge eating, but with the inclusion of the aforementioned compensatory methods (purging, laxative use, or excessive exercise). *Anorexia nervosa* is characterized primarily by intense fear of gaining weight, distorted body image, and restriction of energy intake that (usually but not always) results in low body weight (American Psychiatric Association 2013).

Though binge eating can occur in both eating disorders and food addiction, eating disorders are conceptualized differently than food addiction. Food addiction, as you know, results from overexposure to highly rewarding foods, rewiring your brain in the many ways we have described in chapters 3–5 and resulting in loss of control. Eating disorders, by contrast, result from body image distortions and problematic cultural pressures that lead people to over-restrict their food intake. Societal pressures to be thin often cause adolescent and young adult women to excessively diet or over restrict what and how much they are eating, causing unhealthy weight loss. This can result in rebound binge eating because the body is low on calories or starving. People with eating disorders often undergo vicious cycles of weight fluctuation, bingeing, and purging (Wilcox 2021).

Because their root causes are conceptualized differently, there are also different ways to address and mitigate binge eating problems, depending on whether food addiction or an eating disorder is the primary condition. Importantly, the key goals in the treatment of an eating disorder are to restore proper nutrition (which includes reversing energy deficiency), return to an individualized healthy weight, and address restrictive behaviors so that the drive to binge is extinguished. The primary nutritional goal for food addiction (as you'll soon learn) is to *minimize exposure* to the addictive substance—trigger foods and highly rewarding foods.

Although most of the treatment recommendations are quite similar between food addiction and eating disorders—nutritionally and otherwise—they differ in one key point: food addiction recovery approaches encourage people to *abstain from or significantly reduce consumption* of sugary and ultra-processed foods, whereas eating disorder treatment models *encourage people to learn to eat* sugary and ultra-processed foods in moderation using a "no bad foods" or "all foods in moderation" approach. Therefore, if the wrong person gets the wrong treatment, it could theoretically make their underlying disorder worse.

An important 2020 paper provides guidance to clinicians about how to best decide if an eating disorder is causing someone to score high on the YFAS or if they truly have a food addiction (Wiss and Brewerton 2020). These principles can be used as guidance by you, as well.

First, do you have a history of frequent and restrictive dieting; an intense fear of weight gain; or a history of vomiting, taking laxatives, or overexercising after you binge eat to get rid of calories (Gideon et al. 2016)? Are you underweight, according to BMI charts? Do you score higher than 15 on the EDE-QS (Prnjak et al. 2020)? The EDE-QS is an abbreviated version of the Eating Disorder Examination Questionnaire, and it's used to assess the severity of eating disorders. Space constraints prevent us from being able to provide the full questionnaire here, but it can be found online (see the Resources List at http://www.newharbinger.com/54681).

If your answer is no to all of these, and if you score less than 15 on the EDE-QS but high on the YFAS, you may indeed have a primary food addiction rather than an eating disorder. If your answer is yes to any of these, or if you score more than 15 on the EDE-QS, I recommend you consult a professional trained in the diagnosis of eating disorders (more on how to rope in an eating disorders professional in the bonus chapter on comorbid eating disorders at http://www.newharbinger.com/54681) to find out if you do. Remember too that anorexia nervosa can occur in someone who is normal or overweight, too: if you've been restricting your food intake or engaging in extreme dieting behavior, please see a qualified mental healthcare provider for an assessment right away to be sure you don't need eating disorder treatment.

The second factor to consider as you try to figure out whether you have true food addiction is whether or not you struggle with other addictive behaviors, which may indicate increased susceptibility to food addiction due to shared traits like impulsivity or sensitivity to withdrawal. Do you have a history of an addiction yourself (including caffeine and nicotine)? Is there a history of addictions in your family?

If yes, food addiction is more likely, although if you said yes, it doesn't mean you might not still also have an eating disorder. If no, it does not rule out food addiction, but it lowers the likelihood that food addiction is present.

If you do end up consulting a trained eating disorders professional to find out whether or not you have an eating disorder, and the professional says you do, what does that say about whether or not you have food addiction and how to proceed with the recommendations in this book? There are two possibilities.

It's possible that you *only* have an eating disorder and that you don't have a food addiction (and that the eating disorder, not food addiction, is causing your YFAS score to be high). In this case, evidence-based eating disorder treatment alone might completely resolve your food addiction symptoms.

However, you might instead have *both* a food addiction *and* an eating disorder. Recall that food addiction can also cause eating disorder symptoms. For instance, you might begin restricting your intake of food and excessively dieting in reaction to a loss of control from food addiction; your food addiction symptoms may have preceded your eating disorder symptoms (Wiss 2022a). If this is the case for you, it's possible that treatment in an eating disorders model of care, without supplemental food addiction treatment, won't be enough to get you well. If you think you have both an eating disorder and food addiction, we'll talk much more about what you can do about it in the bonus chapter on comorbidities at http://www.newharbinger.com/54681.

Be aware, too, that severely restricting your calorie intake (anorexia nervosa) or engaging in compensatory measures (bulimia nervosa) can cause life-threatening medical consequences. If you've recently been engaging in these behaviors, please seek help from a trained eating disorders provider or an experienced medical provider right away.

Other Considerations

There are several other considerations for you to keep in mind as we dive into the matter of what to do about food addiction.

Medical Issues

Many patients with food addiction also want to lose weight. You'll soon hear how I believe this should not be a primary goal (chapter 7), as putting it front and center can derail efforts to stabilize the many other distressing symptoms of food addiction. That said, assessment for medical consequences of excess body weight is important (mobility problems, surgical issues that need treatment, and so forth) and might influence treatment planning as well.

Mental Health Issues

You may also want to undergo screening using validated clinical scales and/or more intensive clinical assessment by a trained professional for comorbid mental health issues that often travel with eating disorders and food addiction. A history of trauma could influence your treatment planning, especially if you have developed PTSD. Other psychiatric diagnoses—including anxiety, depression, bipolar disorder, and ADHD, to name a few—should be identified and treated, as these problems can make recovery much harder if not addressed. Your treatment plan should include evidence-based treatment (medications, psychotherapy, and the like) for the disorder in question, because this will help you recover from food addiction faster. In addition, consider your use of other substances, including nicotine, alcohol, cannabis, and other illicit drugs. People with food addiction have a higher risk of addiction to other substances, and not addressing other addictions will almost certainly undermine your progress. In the Resources List available at http://www.newharbinger.com/54681, I've listed my favorite screening tools for depression, anxiety, ADHD, childhood trauma, PTSD, and alcohol use disorder.

After all this, if you feel pretty confident that you have food addiction, and have thought about whether an eating disorder might be contributing (and addressed it by accessing support, if so), you're ready to move on! In the next chapters, you're going to learn how reducing your exposure to and consumption of highly rewarding food and intervening in the patterns of thought and behavior with a number of new skills is going to help you break free!

Also remember to access the comorbidities chapter at http://www.newharbinger.com/54681 if you have any concern at all for an eating disorder, as it contains invaluable information on management and treatment.

CHAPTER 7

The Sacrifice Is the Promise

"When you really have the thing and then get treatment for the thing, it's pretty incredible how it works."

—Molly Carmel, *Food Junkies Podcast*

So you filled out the YFAS, and you think you have food addiction, and you feel that overexposure to highly rewarding food has adversely affected your brain, making you feel out of control. So, now what? How do you stop the cravings, obsessions, and unwanted behaviors? How do you rewire your brain back to health? For those of us facing food addiction, panic often ensues because it is not a simple, quick fix.

In this chapter, you'll learn that the foundation of a food addiction recovery plan is to stop or significantly reduce consumption of highly rewarding foods. If you do so, your brain's neurochemistry will come back into balance. It may sound daunting at first, but I hope to convince you that by making a big change like this, you'll experience abundance, not deprivation. And once you start the process, it will be an upward spiral. You may need some motivation and hope to get through the harder days, but once you get over the hump, things will truly start looking up more and more every day.

Limiting Intake Rewires the Brain

I'm not suggesting you eliminate your exposure to most highly rewarding foods to torture you. The bad news that these foods have many adverse effects on the brain has a silver lining: if you reduce your brain's exposure to these toxic substances, it will rewire itself back to health. The end goal is to heal your brain. The longer you significantly reduce exposure or abstain, the more your brain will heal, and the more your obsessions and related unhelpful behaviors will become a problem of the past. Your neurochemistry is fixable! You will also address the problem at its source, way further upstream than things like weight-loss medications or bariatric surgery, for example.

Research has established that for people with substance addictions, eliminating exposure to the substance promotes brain healing (Wilcox 2021; Volkow et al. 2002; Wilcox et al. 2013)! Remember the concept of extinction from chapter 1, the process by which we unlearn a behavior that has been acquired through conditioned learning? By avoiding triggers and their associated rewards, the brain's response to these cues gradually weakens because the outcome that reinforced the behavior—the gratification of consuming highly rewarding food—is no longer present (Bouton, Maren, and McNally 2021).

Most people in recovery from addictions will vouch that, in their experience, they can feel the extinction happen, and that the longer they minimize exposure to whatever the problem toxin is, the less sensitive they are to cues. Most long-term ex-smokers will tell you that in the past, the smell of smoke or the feeling of irritability would instantly cause them to crave a cigarette, but that now, they don't even think about smoking anymore. They even feel disgusted when they see someone smoking. The cues have lost their triggering power. The smoking behavior has been extinguished. This will happen for you with the highly rewarding foods, too.

While there's no formal research on changes in our brains when we abstain from or significantly cut our consumption of highly rewarding food, we know a lot about the healing that occurs when we reduce or stop our use of other substances of abuse. Studies show that shrunken brains get bigger; impulse control and emotion regulation circuits come back online; the neurochemistry underlying the opponent process discussed in chapter 4 reverses so we are no longer tolerant or susceptible to withdrawal; our moods improve; and the density of dopamine receptors normalizes in the cortex and striatum, improving our impulse control and decision making (Wilcox

2021; Volkow et al. 2002; Wilcox et al. 2013). Also, remember how even a little bit of our drug of choice can cause dopamine release, which increases our motivation for more (chapter 2)? This, too, will be a risk of the past, if we are no longer regularly using the reward.

We also know that brain function normalizes when people with obesity lose weight (Wilcox 2021). In a society that valorizes thinness, we're often tempted to read this as being the result of weight loss; my guess is that it may have more to do with participants cutting out highly rewarding food in their weight-loss plans.

The long and short of it is this: all the problems that you learned about in chapters 3–5 go away, with time. Seriously.

The Foundation of a Recovery Plan

If you're anything like me, your anxiety is still running high. Does this mean you never get to eat cake and cookies again? It will depend on your personal situation and chemical makeup. Does this mean you have to eat lettuce and chicken for the rest of your life? No, trust me. I want you to have a food plan that is abundant, beautiful, tasty, and full of as much variety as possible. We'll get much more into food plans in the next chapter. I'll also give you plenty of tools to support you as you make this big change, in chapters 10–12.

Meanwhile, part of what you're intuiting is correct: I will be advocating for you to cut out or significantly reduce your intake of highly rewarding foods. There are lots of ways to approach this and personalize it. So, what that will mean for you may not be what it means for me, or Sara, or Jen, for example. It's also true that many of us who have recovered from food addiction couldn't possibly have imagined letting go of our most beloved highly rewarding foods when we began the recovery journey. We also struggled to make the changes stick. But once we were able to—for even a few weeks—we really started to reap the benefits. And over a lifetime, we come to be amazed by how much peace we get from avoiding the foods that controlled us most.

As Clarissa and Molly of *Food Junkies* have observed in their practices, people start to feel they have turned a corner in terms of cravings and mood by about three weeks of adhering to the food plan (if it's the right plan for them). They suggest giving yourself 30–45 days for your brain to recalibrate before you decide whether an approach like this, or any particular food plan, is right for you.

It's also worth recognizing what you'll look forward to gaining from recovery. Besides a brain that works better and a renewed sense of personal control, what else can you expect? Podcast guests Susan Peirce Thompson (Thompson 2022), author of *Bright Line Eating*, and David Wiss (Wiss 2021a, 2021b), emphasize neutrality around food and inner peace. Other benefits of recovery, which I can attest to experiencing myself, include higher energy, greater self-confidence, more consistency of mood and character, and a greater sense of well-being, as well as relief from food hangovers and the intense, sometimes debilitating obsessions and cravings. Body image often improves in recovery too, regardless of weight loss. Finally, recovery brings improved physical health—be it better blood glucose control, lower cholesterol levels, improved cognitive function, or increased mobility or fitness, just to name a few. A lot of people in active food addiction have lost the ability to feel hunger and satiety signals—and thus, when they try "intuitive eating" practices, those doesn't work for them. But for many of us, avoiding highly rewarding food restores our ability to feel hunger and fullness again and eat in attuned or intuitive ways! In recovery, "all people can learn to start trusting their bodies," Kim Dennis says on the podcast (Dennis 2021a).

A Motivational Time Out

When I started down this path, I knew in my bones that I needed to completely cut out high-sugar, ultra-processed cakes and cookies because I had already learned from long experience that just one cookie would lead to a full-on binge—if not right away, definitely within a few days. You may be feeling similarly about your most problematic foods.

The first step in 12-step programs is, "I am powerless over drug X and my life has become unmanageable." At first glance, this introductory step may appear dreary and hopeless. It may feel unfair that some of us don't seem to have trouble eating one cookie without a disaster ensuing. However, the truth—as many of us have discovered—is that the sooner we accept our true biochemical situation, and stop denying it, the faster we can figure out how to get well.

In the case of food addiction, acceptance of whatever our personal reality is greases the wheels to becoming craving-free. Acceptance is NOT the same as agreeing or giving up though—when we accept we have food addiction, it doesn't mean that we should just keep eating and eating because there's nothing we can do about it. It just means that we need to address our problem in a way that acknowledges our limitations—for example, by setting an intention to avoid the foods that are causing our problem in the first place. Acceptance is actually a gift.

Exercise: Benefits and Drawbacks

As you consider taking this leap, I'd like to have you examine a series of questions from an evidence-based therapy for addiction treatment called motivational interviewing (Miller and Rollnick 2023).

1. How important is it, on a scale of 1–10, to stop or significantly reduce your consumption of highly rewarding food—the foods you listed from the exercise you did at the end of chapter 2?

2. As you consider making this change of cutting out highly rewarding food:

    What are some benefits of making the change?

    What are some benefits of not making the change?

    What are some of the downsides/costs of making the change?

    What are some of the downsides/costs of not making the change?

3. After thinking about these factors, now how important is it, on a scale of 1–10, to stop or significantly reduce your consumption of highly rewarding foods? Why is it a _____ and not a 1? (This last question will help pull out reasons why you think it's important to reduce your consumption of highly rewarding foods.)

Weight Loss Is Not the Primary Goal

David Wiss once told me that if he was going to write a book, he'd title it "Food Addiction: When It's Not About the Weight." Although following the strategies outlined in this book may lead you to release some weight, over-prioritizing weight loss tends to hinder progress in overcoming food addiction.

Calorie counting, dieting, and overexercising with the intent to burn calories is not helpful for people with food addiction. When we overfocus on weight and weight loss, we often undereat and we get hungry. Restrictive eating is bad for food addiction recovery because it significantly increases the risk of bingeing (Wiss 2021a, 2021b; Dennis 2021a; DesMaisons 2022; Dennis 2021b). Also, if we don't see pounds come off fast, shame and self-blame increase, our body image deteriorates, and we restrict even more. This is one place where modern-day food addiction providers and eating disorder specialists are 100 percent in alignment: *dieting is no good.*

I can actually hear my old self screaming, "But wait! I'm here to lose weight!" I fully validate and empathize with your desire to release weight if you're one of these people (we've all been there). But I ask you to try to let that goal go for now, put your faith in this principle—that it's not about the weight—and just see what happens. If you're like most of us, you've tried throngs of other approaches already, many of which are premised on losing weight. And none of it has given you what you were looking for.

Hunger and calorie deficiency fuels all kinds of addictive behavior by causing changes in our brain's reward circuitry. First, the high we experience from highly rewarding food is greater when we're hungry, fasting, or anticipating scarcity, studies show. Second, the conditioning process is more robust when we are in a nutritional deficit—calorie deprivation or hunger makes the dopamine surge greater and induces more reinforcement and more learning through conditioning. Third, environmental cues light up our reward circuitry more when we are hungry or calorically deprived (Wilcox 2021). Fourth, reductions in glucose levels in our brains can reduce our impulse control and capacity to solve problems, because our neurons need energy to carry out their tasks (Kahneman 2011). Fifth, excess dieting and food restriction increases cortisol levels, which feels like stress to our bodies. High cortisol levels are also correlated with insomnia, increased craving, and greater brain activation to food cues. Sixth, hunger exacerbates negative mood states and can intensify the withdrawal symptoms that many of us experience when we let go of highly rewarding food, increasing insomnia, irritability, anxiety, and craving. Seventh, when we are hungry, the homeostatic system stops keeping the hedonic system under wraps. Remember the information in chapter 3 about how insulin and leptin, which go up when we eat, reduce homeostatic eating? It turns out these neurohormones also dampen rewarding dopamine activity in the striatum and reduce hedonic eating too! Ghrelin, the neurohormone that stimulates appetite and is released during energy deficiency, also amplifies dopamine and endogenous opioid activity in brain areas of the reward network, promoting hedonic eating. Therefore, when we're hungry, and insulin and leptin levels are low, and ghrelin levels high, our risk of being triggered by cues is especially high (Wilcox 2021).

Instead of dieting, your brain needs to be nurtured back to health with enough nutritious food, especially in the first six to twelve months. This is a key component of rewiring your brain because your reward system will be less sensitive, your emotional stability will improve, and you will have better impulse control. Without adequate nourishment, you'll struggle much harder than you need to.

You may want to release weight to address certain health problems or just to improve a sense of well-being. This is entirely valid. A long-term goal of weight loss is absolutely worthwhile. And if you have that long-term goal, know that the vast majority of people who get into recovery from food addiction *do* end up releasing weight as a side-benefit if they start out overweight or obese. In fact, letting go of highly rewarding foods might, over time, reduce our set point, meaning that our body naturally gravitates toward being at a lower weight (Guyenet 2022a, 2022b). This is a shift experienced by many people with food addiction (including me!). But this weight release may not happen right away, and everyone who experiences it has a different trajectory. Patience will be key.

If the idea of letting go of weight loss (for now) terrifies you, you're not alone. Molly Carmel says an "addiction to dieting" is harder to get rid of than addiction to sugar or flour. Our society fuels our desires for thinness, and toxic diet culture is all around us: in the doctor's office, in advertisements, in well-meaning advice from friends (Carmel 2021). Even if trying to lose weight is not in our best interest in the short run, unhelpful desires to restrict our calorie intake can be as easily fueled as those for highly rewarding food. If you experience distress as a result of body image dissatisfaction, and if you feel like you need some skills to help you deemphasize weight loss as a goal, please see the handout at http://www.newharbinger.com/54681.

Your Personal Recovery Goals

So, if it's not going to be all about weight loss, what will be your goals for your recovery, then? What are you hoping to achieve? Being clear about this from the start can help you when you find that motivation wanes.

Exercise: Clarifying Your Goals

Circle (or write in your journal) any of the goals listed below that resonate with you:

- a life free of food obsession and cravings
- a life free from the endless cycle of restriction and excess
- achieving life goals beyond food- and body-related aims
- increasing your energy to support your friends, family, and loved ones
- freedom from the manipulation of the food industry
- lower depression, irritability, and anxiety symptoms
- higher inner peace
- better concentration and attention
- reconnection to true hunger/fullness cues
- better body image
- neutrality around food
- enhanced decision making

- higher self-esteem and confidence
- a more optimistic outlook
- better connection in personal relationships

Next, write ten of your own personal recovery goals down in sentence format.

Example:

I want to have neutrality around food.

I want to stop obsessing over food.

I want to improve my blood sugar control.

Next, rate yourself on your success with each goal, *today*. Convert each goal to an affirmative statement (see below) and rate it on a scale of 1–5, with 1 – None of the time, 2 – Rarely, 3 – Some of the time, 4 – Often, 5 – All of the time

Example:

I have neutrality around food (3 – Some of the time)

I don't obsess over food (1 – None of the time)

I have adequate blood sugar control (2 – Rarely)

We'll come back to this personal goal list later.

Sources of Hope and Motivation

Making and sustaining behavior change is challenging. Most of us find we frequently need a dose of inspiration—especially during early recovery, when the justifications are scurrying around our brains at all hours.

Joining a recovery community can help boost your positive outlook and enhance your motivation. Meeting people further along in recovery who are happy and free will energize you! In recovery communities, you can meet people who will tell you what's worked for them, teach you tips and tricks, give you new ideas for recovery goals, and understand what you are doing and support you.

Twelve-step programs such as AA, Narcotics Anonymous, and others are popular for people with substance use disorders. These groups give participants a structured way to boost spirituality, understand their own psychological and social patterns, and learn skills and tools to facilitate the changes they want to make in themselves. They don't cost anything! And when it comes to alcohol and other substances, these meetings work, studies show (Kelly 2024; Wilcox, Pearson, and Tonigan 2015; Wilcox and Tonigan 2018).

Although the program offered in this book isn't directly 12-step based, and the studies are yet to be done on whether or not 12-step programs help promote eating behavior change, know that there are also several well-established food-based 12-step programs, including Overeaters Anonymous (OA). You might consider checking a meeting out for yourself. Schedules for online and in-person meetings in your area are readily available online.

Note that while most general OA meetings are flexible, some 12-step programs for food issues do presume particular food plans, which may or may not mesh with the one you'll be guided to develop for yourself in this book to learn to eat abundantly while helping your brain stabilize. You'll hear more about this caveat in later chapters.

Another free way to get a boost in your motivation is to listen to podcasts! If this appeals to you, start with *The Food Junkies Podcast* https://www.foodjunkiespodcast.com. Here, food addiction researchers, investigative reporters, public policy experts, leaders in nutrition science, professors in the social sciences, addiction neuroscientists and treatment experts, eating disorders experts, food addiction treatment experts, people in recovery, and more bounce ideas off one another and share riveting personal and professional stories about food addiction recovery and science. Clarissa, Molly, and Vera are spectacular interviewers: open-minded, endlessly curious, and warm. There also seems to be a significant amount of overlap and convergence in what's being discussed by guests on the show—which is heartening because it means that, collectively, they may be onto something.

Community can also be built through social media and other forms of technology, such as evidence-based apps. These are easy to access and sometimes free. Also, I strongly recommend you consider reading some memoirs and/or listening to recovery stories. Recommended social media, apps, memoirs, and recovery stories are available at http://www.newharbinger.com/54681.

In sum, I hope that now you feel more convinced that *the sacrifice is the promise*. I hope you're also feeling excited that you have some recovery goals in mind and you're in a good place to dive into the next phase of your recovery—crafting your food plan—which will be the subject of the next chapter.

CHAPTER 8

What To Eat? Food Plans

"Food can be used to rewire the brain."

—David Wiss, *Food Junkies Podcast*

Now that you have set some goals and understand why both avoiding highly rewarding food and eating enough are essential parts of recovery, it's time to make a *food plan*, which will serve as your daily guide for what to eat every day.

The three principles of a food addiction recovery food plan are to 1) eat plenty of high-quality nourishing food, 2) minimize or stop eating highly rewarding foods, including your own personal trigger foods, and 3) portioning so that you are eating the right amount of food while aligning the macronutrient composition (fat, carbs, protein) of your meals to your dietary requirements. Stated simply, a food plan will give you structure around what to eat, what not to eat, and how much to eat.

- *Lucy's Story, Part 2*

    Lucy struggled with weight issues and binge eating her entire life. She'd tried an intensive outpatient program for binge eating disorder, medication for depression, Overeaters Anonymous meeting attendance, and multiple "diets." Her cravings for certain foods, especially sweets, were often insatiable. One day, she went to the doctor, who told her she was on the road to developing type 2 diabetes. Scared, she embraced the concept of food addiction and adopted a food plan involving no sugar, no ultra-processed foods, no flour, plenty of protein and vegetables, and *five meals a day. She felt irritable, restless, and foggy for a couple weeks, and experienced some mood swings. She sought support from her friends in OA and by week three, her food cravings plummeted. By month six, she was able to taper off the medication she'd been taking for depression and her blood glucose levels were normal again—no sign of diabetes. Today, two years later, she has lost 15 percent of her body weight. She still uses the guidelines she began following with her initial food plans, and she no longer thinks much about the food quantities she's eating. She just eats until she's full.*

Principle 1: Eat Plenty of High Quality, Nourishing Food

The first principle is to *regularly eat plenty of quality food*, which means eating frequent, minimally processed meals with ample amounts of whole foods—vegetables, fruit, lean protein, fiber, healthy fats—which naturally contain high levels of important vitamins and micronutrients. These nutrient-dense foods will stabilize emotion regulation and impulse control circuits, reducing the power of food cues to veer you off course and making it easier to stay away from your problem foods.

What Is Nourishing Food?

Nourishing food is real food, usually identifiable as food "without a label," says Robert Lustig (2021). It's also whole food. Whole foods are nonprocessed natural foods—think about the fruits, vegetables, legumes, fungi, nuts, and seeds you can just eat with minimal preparation. These foods are most similar to our hunter-gatherer ancestors' diet to which our brains are biologically adapted. Unlike highly rewarding foods, whole foods feed us without fueling our cravings.

A diet rich in fresh, whole foods, protein, and fiber is the backbone of a food addiction-oriented food plan (DesMaisons 2022; Avena 2021; Carmel 2021; Bikman 2022; Kaplan 2023; Dennis 2021a; Wiss 2021a; Nestle 2021; Wiss 2021b; Dennis 2021b). Fruits and veggies of all kinds are unambiguously recommended. Whole grains; legumes like lentils; and seeds and healthy fats, like avocados, are also often good choices, although some people decide to limit their consumption of some whole grains if they trigger craving. Protein can be either high quality animal-based protein or through plant sources like tofu. Ben Bikman, author of *Why We Get Sick,* recommends eating 1.5 grams of protein per kilogram of body weight—primarily animal protein, such as meat, eggs, and dairy (Bikman 2022). I recommend 1 gram per kilogram of body weight as a more realistic starting target (which will be reflected in the food plan below). Studies show that protein and fiber are satiating and reinstate the balance between appetite-regulating hormones like leptin, ghrelin, and insulin (Wilcox 2021).

Eating a wide variety of foods is important too (Nestle 2021; Kaplan 2023). Variety prevents overuse of particular foods, which prevents conditioning (chapter 3). To emphasize the importance of variety, David Katz, internal medicine physician and coauthor of *How to Eat,* has coined the term "tastebud rehab." Katz says familiarity is "one of the most potent drivers of dietary preference"; when we repeatedly eat the same highly rewarding foods, our taste buds become desensitized to that taste due to tolerance, resulting in overconsumption (Katz 2023). It takes fourteen days to recalibrate our reward system after removing something we've eaten regularly, like sugar. At that point, our taste buds will be easily stimulated again—fresh blueberries or strawberries is all the sweet we'll ever need.

The other reason to eat a wide variety of nourishing foods is to replenish micronutrients. Recall how overexposure to highly palatable foods leads rats in laboratories to opt out of rat chow, their version of nourishing food (Reichelt 2023); you too may be in a nutrient-depleted state, impairing your impulse control, mood, and irritability levels (Wilcox 2021). James Greenblatt, psychiatrist and author of *Integrative Medicine for Alzheimer's,* says "sugar is a nutritional vacuum"(Greenblatt 2022). Omega-3 fatty acids, vitamin D, B12, iron, zinc, and magnesium are crucial for optimal mental health, among others (see the Resource List at http://www.newharbinger.com/54681 for more detailed information). Research psychologist Bonnie Kaplan believes that we shouldn't overfocus on individual micronutrients because they work synergistically. Instead, optimizing all micronutrients with a micronutrient complex improves a variety of mental health parameters, increasing trauma resilience and reducing attention deficit disorder symptoms (Kaplan 2023; Kaplan et al. 2015; Johnstone et al. 2022). While a high-quality micronutrient complex like EMPowerplus (https://www.truehope.com/research) is an option, the healthiest approach to restore our micronutrients is through our diet, she says.

Principle 2: Minimize or Stop Eating Highly Rewarding Foods

The second principle is to *cut out most or all highly rewarding food.*

One straightforward way to do this is to use sugar content to draw that line. Most people with food addiction have issues with high-sugar foods. It also follows the science: sugar is addictive (Avena 2021). If you avoid any foods that have sugar in one of its 262 forms (see the Resources List at http://www.newharbinger.com/54681) listed in the top four ingredients, and stop adding any of the 262 kinds of sugars to homemade foods, you will have removed a significant portion of likely culprits. Remember: fresh fruit and non-sugary carbohydrates (potatoes, rice, pasta, shredded wheat) don't count as sugar, so they don't need to be avoided, unless you identify one or several as a personal trigger food.

Cutting out sugar in this way was key for my recovery. Although the addicted parts of me fought the approach initially, the advantages—that it felt simple and didn't require me to think much about what was alright and what wasn't—won out in the end. Once I'd finally stopped, it did give me a feeling that I had gone through a quantum change, with the cravings practically vanishing.

An alternate or complementary approach is to develop your personal list of triggering foods and to use this personalized list to help you make decisions day-to-day about what to avoid.

Sometimes I find my partner, Bill, standing next to the kitchen counter in an almost fugue state, eating chips out of a bag, several at a time, sometimes using both hands to feed himself. He often eats until the bag is empty, oblivious to the dogs circling around him, wagging their tails and snorting in delight when the occasional crumb falls. He loves his chips, and his heaven is found in the combination of crunch, salt, carb, and fat. Interestingly, he does not meet the criteria for food addiction according to the YFAS, which I've administered to him. By contrast, I can take or leave chips. It's weird. Although I *do* have food addiction, it's easy for me to have just two or three and then move on. Bill is enthralled with my willpower. But it's not willpower that keeps me from overdoing it. It's just that they're not that interesting to me. Unlike him, my problem foods tend to be sweet, soft, and rich.

Trigger foods vary between individuals. Exposure, genetics, and likely many other variables cause these differences between people. Whereas one person's weakness may be cookies and cake, another might overeat chips and pizza. Some people have trouble with other carbohydrates, like potatoes, pasta, bread, bananas, dates, or popcorn, as examples.

Exercise: **Identify Your Trigger Foods**

This is a guided journaling exercise. Trigger foods include foods you tend to overeat or binge on, foods that you use to regulate your emotions, foods that you have a hard time having "just one bite" of, and the foods whose associated smells, sights, and sounds make you crave.

First, recall the list of higher-risk foods that I presented in chapter 2:

- Sugar, honey, maple syrup, agave, foods produced with added sugar
- Ultra-processed foods
- Foods made at home that you crave, overeat, and/or that have the macronutrient ratios seen in hyperpalatable foods
- Foods on the top of the "addictiveness" list (hamburgers, fries, pizza, cookies, cake, ice cream, chips, and the like), which can often include foods with a high glycemic index
- Soft, low-fiber, "fast-acting" foods
- For some individuals (but not most): dairy, gluten, high-carbohydrate diets, certain fats, and artificial sweeteners

Also recall the list of your personal problem foods you generated in the exercise at the end of chapter 2.

Does anything on these lists make you think of a food item that you should be adding to your trigger food list?

Here are several more questions adopted from a list provided by Sweet Sobriety (https://www.sweetsobriety.ca) and elsewhere (Thompson 2022) that I would like you to journal on.

- Do certain foods affect your energy and/or mood?
- Are there foods that you crave excessively or have difficulty controlling your intake of?
- Do you notice any obsessive thoughts after seeing or consuming a specific food?
- Do you often feel sluggish or experience brain fog after eating certain meals or snacks?
- Are there any foods that you tend to overeat even when you're not hungry?
- Do you feel angry or fearful about giving up specific foods? If so, why? Which reasons seem wise, and which seem to be justifications, now that you see them on paper?
- Do you use certain foods for emotional comfort or boredom relief?
- What foods trigger emotional responses in you?

After doing some writing on the above, add to your tentative list of trigger foods. Then go through a week eating as usual and see what else you learn, adjusting your trigger food list as needed.

Know that this list will likely morph over time as you learn more about yourself through the process of recovery. However, try not to make changes too often. After you've drafted your initial food plan and begun to implement it, give it at least a week of thought before adding or subtracting any items to your list.

Sometimes trigger foods can be hard to identify: people will adhere to a food plan for several weeks and experience little to no reduction in cravings. This might be because there is a hidden trigger food in the food plan—something that a person doesn't particularly crave but that is fueling their addictive circuitry in some way. For example, caffeine, which initially suppresses appetite, may be a trigger for us when it wears off (Werdell 2022). Food diaries help to identify hidden trigger foods.

Finally, when you do decide to remove a particular food item from your food plan, don't say I *can't* eat these foods (be it a food with high sugar or a personal trigger food); instead, say I *choose* not to eat these foods, to reinforce your autonomy.

Principle 3: Eat the Right Amount of Food

Remember how important it is for your brain chemistry to eat enough (chapter 7)? This is the third principle of a food plan—to make sure you're getting enough calories from your foods so that you're not hungry and that you are getting adequate ratios of macronutrients (fat, protein, and carbohydrate). Through portioning, you will learn to put enough food on your plate and in your stomach. Portioning will also help you understand what constitutes overeating, as in the first year of recovery you may occasionally have urges to eat higher-than-helpful quantities of nourishing food, to quell the cravings.

Most of us in early recovery find we need at least some structure and guidance about healthy portioning. We often lean toward undereating out of the gate because we want to lose weight. But remember, it's best to let the idea of weight loss go—especially in the first few months, as appropriate portioning will help you rewire your brain and make it easier to make sustainable food choices. Furthermore, a lot of us need to learn what the appropriate proportions of carbohydrate, protein, and fat are. I'll be giving you guidelines about this in the food plan section.

For portioning, many of us buy a food scale and/or use measuring cups or spoons to stay within the intended quantity ranges. Some of us weigh and measure only initially; others of us keep weighing and measuring years into recovery because it gives us a sense of peace to relinquish the guesswork.

Another reason to set some boundaries around our proportions at any point in recovery is to prevent "carb creep" (Unwin 2021b). When we let go of highly rewarding foods, some of us can subconsciously drift into overeating the carbohydrates we still have in our food plan. Or we'll find ourselves crafting never-before-problematic, hyperpalatable combinations to replace the loss of highly rewarding foods, such as potato with butter and salt, or brown rice with melted cheese. Without a "how much" and "how often" set of boundaries around certain foods, the drift may turn into a tidal wave and we start to binge on the new problem food.

That said, some of us don't need to weigh or measure at all. I've met some people who simply needed to stop eating sugar, after which all the cravings went away and they were able to know intuitively when they had eaten enough or needed to eat more.

Over time, as you adhere to these three principles, you may find that your need for portioning diminishes. You may start to regain—or for the first time, develop—the ability to feel true hunger and true fullness. You might start to gain trust in these bodily signals to decide when to start and stop eating, and adopt more intuitive eating principles.

Your newfound ability to use intrinsic hunger and fullness cues to regulate your eating will be the result of several positive physiological changes in the homeostatic system. First, when your eating stabilizes, you will become sensitive to insulin and leptin again. When your body says you're full, you'll feel it. Second, the vagus nerve will come back online (recall that high-sugar, ultra-processed food impairs vagus nerve function from chapter 3) with removal of these foods, which will allow your stretch receptors in your gut to communicate with your brain after you eat.

What about meal frequencies? Most people with food addiction end up doing best with regular meals. Three meals a day with four to six hours between, plus a snack or two, is where most people land. You can discuss this with a dietitian or nutritionist, or you can just try out the food plans we suggest and adapt them to your needs.

Also, hunger and withdrawal from highly rewarding food can cause insomnia. For this reason, many food-addiction professionals, including Clarissa and Molly of *Food Junkies*, recommend incorporating a "constitutional" or a "metabolic" into the food plan, which is a small meal at bedtime—usually a complex, slow-release carbohydrate or a high-protein food, such as a potato, chickpeas, or frozen fruit with kefir; or foods rich in tryptophan—the precursor to serotonin and melatonin—such as a few nuts or Greek yogurt (DesMaisons 2022; Wiss 2021a, 2021b; Reichelt 2023).

Note that fasting approaches, such as intermittent fasting, are likely not going to turn out to be helpful for most people with food addiction. Although studies show intermittent fasting reduces insulin resistance and possibly even cravings by producing satiating, brain-healthy and anti-inflammatory ketones (Bikman 2022), hunger during the fasting portion or after fasting has ended (when ketone levels plummet) could easily trigger someone with addictive wiring. Hunger triggers our addiction neural circuitry, and eating nothing for large blocks of time is like throwing kindling on a fire.

Volume Addiction

Not all people regain the ability to eat intuitively, even after many months of sticking with a food plan rooted in the principles in this chapter. For a small subset of people, binge eating—even on foods with a low dopamine hit like broccoli—persists even after all problematic foods have been eliminated. This may be a case where the act of eating itself is a reinforcing factor that sustains the behavior, not just the biochemical effect of a particular food.

If you have volume addiction, there are several possible reasons you do, from a physiological perspective. You could have lingering issues with your homeostatic system, specifically leptin, insulin, and ghrelin release and sensitivity, or problems with your stretch receptors or vagus nerve (Wilcox 2021; Tarman 2019; Tarman 2024). Or, deficient oxytocin signaling could be to blame (Moberg 2022), as oxytocin, which inhibits carbohydrate intake (Olszewski et al. 2010), is released after stomach distention to signal satiety, and inadequate signals may explain the need to keep eating. Another theory attributes volume addiction to alterations in serotonin sensitivity, suggesting that eating large quantities may release more serotonin, providing a soothing, stress-reducing effect (Ifland 2021).

In the end though, our understanding of the biology of volume addiction—and whether or not it is a valid clinical syndrome—remains uncertain. These explanations are theoretical, and more research to figure out treatment protocols for people with food addiction and volume addiction is definitely warranted.

In the meantime, if you're in early- or mid- recovery and you still want to overeat broccoli, don't make too much of it. If you're in late recovery (that is, you've been in recovery longer than a year) and you're still experiencing desires to overeat after problematic foods have been eliminated, it may mean that you do have some volume addiction issues. Continued portion control is our most powerful weapon against volume addiction. Also, Clarissa and Molly teach mindfulness-based exercises developed through the lens of somatic-based approaches and polyvagal theory (Biasetti 2022; Lewis-Marlow 2023) to their clients with volume addiction, which can be used pre- or post-meal (handouts available online at http://www.newharbinger.com/54681).

The Evidence

What's the proof that these principles work? Three important studies have been done for the treatment of food addiction, and between them, they provide supporting evidence for the food plan options I am about to recommend.

The biggest and most recent study, TRACE (Targeted Research for Addictive and Compulsive Eating), randomized 175 individuals to one of three interventions.

- The active intervention used a personalized approach, first helping participants identify personal problem areas from both nutritional and personality perspectives, and then providing personalized nutritional plans to increase energy percentages gained from "core foods" (fruits, veggies, whole grains, dairy, meat) and reduce energy gained from "non-core foods" (junk/processed foods). Participants also received a personalized skills plan to address their personality vulnerabilities via telehealth sessions.

- In the passive intervention, participants completed the same program via a self-help approach.

- Finally, a control group was asked to follow their usual dietary pattern for six months.

The active group was five times more likely to have a reduction in food addiction scores compared to the control group. Passive group participants also showed significant improvement in food addiction scores compared to the control group. Depression scores improved in both the active and passive group (Skinner et al. 2024).

In a second study, 103 participants were treated in an online program by three teams (UK, Sweden, North America) with a whole-food-based, low-carbohydrate education and psychosocial support. There was no personalization; a general dietary approach was provided, similar to the principles discussed in this chapter. Across sites, mental well-being improved from baseline to week 10–14 (the three sites had variable lengths of treatment) and food addiction symptoms and weight diminished, with a mean weight loss of 2.45 kg across sites (Unwin et al. 2022). Interestingly, the North American site had the most dropout and least robust treatment response of the three. Jen Unwin, first author of the study and author of *Fork in the Road*, theorizes that increased cultural pressure and advertising surrounding highly rewarding food in the US and Canada contributes to this issue (Unwin 2021b).

The third study had a much smaller sample size. Five participants with binge eating and a desire for weight loss, four of whom had food addiction, went on a very low-calorie ketogenic diet. After the dietary intervention, which lasted 5–7 weeks, all participants were free of binge eating and food addiction symptoms, with an average body weight reduction between 5–12 percent. Participants were switched to a low-calorie diet for 11–21 weeks, after which average weight loss was 13 percent. Reductions in food addiction, binge eating, and weight were maintained (Rostanzo et al. 2021).

The last two studies both showed that low-carbohydrate approaches might be of benefit for people with food addiction. They differed from one another in their sample sizes, and the restrictiveness of the food plan: the study that used a ketogenic diet should be the least emphasized because of its smaller size and the theoretical increased risk of causing harm (eating disorders) by a more restrictive diet.

The first study was unique in that it used a personalized food plan. It was randomized and controlled as well, distinguishing it from the other two, but it did not directly test one food plan against another.

All three studies showed that food addiction symptoms can remit with a combination of support and a dietary intervention that follows our three key principles: avoid highly rewarding food, eat plenty of nourishing food, and portion appropriately.

That said, we definitely need more research in this area. No randomized controlled trials testing a food addiction food plan against standard nutritional therapy have yet been done (which is the kind of research needed for a treatment to be truly evidence-based), nor do we yet know which food plans are best for which people.

The Plans

Now I will offer you three different starter food plans to choose from, developed in collaboration with Clarissa Kennedy and Amy Reichelt. Each plan adheres to the three principles for food addiction food plans outlined in this chapter and allows for personalization. If you're not sure which to try, I'd suggest the Stage 1 food plan first. If you struggle to control cravings or stick to the plan after 3–4 weeks, it's likely there is a triggering food in there, so consider Stage 2. If that doesn't work, go to Stage 3, the low-carb food plan.

Another way to decide what food plan to start with is to go back to chapter 6, where you filled out the YFAS. Did you score mild, moderate, or severe? If it was mild, start with Stage 2; if moderate, start with Stage 2; if severe, start with Stage 3.

While those of us with food addiction are similar in our sensitized brain circuitry, we each have unique genetics, food triggers, and personal physical and mental health histories, as we discussed in the trigger foods exercise in this chapter. We also have varied cultural origins and financial resources. For these reasons, I advocate for an individualized treatment approach to food-plan development, as do many other specialists in the field (Wiss 2021a; Dennis 2021a; Wiss 2021b, 2023; Dennis 2021b), including Molly and Clarissa of *Food Junkies*. For you, reading this book as a self-help resource, you'll likely need to do some experimentation and refinement on your own (or seek guidance from a qualified professional as discussed in the bonus chapters at http://www.newharbinger.com/54681). Also, make sure to integrate skills from chapters 10–12 and consider getting involved in a recovery community, which will reduce your cravings, improve your mood, and increase your impulse control, in the same way that eating enough and avoiding highly rewarding food will.

These food plans are designed to support you in abstaining from highly rewarding food so that your body and mind can heal and you can get closer to your recovery goals. Pick the food plan that best aids you in doing so! Know that in the future, after some weeks or months once the cravings abate, you may (or may not!) be able to step down to a more permissive food plan.

Stage 1 Food Plan (Most Permissive Plan)

Breakfast

1.5–2 protein

1–1.5 starch/carbohydrate

1–2 fats

4–10 oz. vegetable

Lunch

1.5–2 protein

1–2 fats

6–12 oz. fruit

Dinner

1.5–2 protein

1–1.5 starch or carbohydrate

1–2 fats

4–10 oz. vegetable

Metabolic: (evening, optional, before bed)

0.5–1.5 protein

4–6 oz. veg/fruit OR .5 starch/carbohydrate

1 fat

1 Fat (1 TBSP unless otherwise noted):

Olive, canola, sesame, or coconut oil

Butter or ghee

Animal fat (such as tallow or lard)

Mayonnaise made with avocado oil

Pesto sauce

Primal Kitchen or Chosen Foods mayo or dressing

1/2 avocado

1 oz. nuts

4 oz. olives

Seeds (pumpkin, sunflower)

2 Tbsp chia seeds

¼ cup sour cream

**Nut butter

1 Protein:

Poultry 4 oz.

Pork 4 oz.

Beef 4 oz.

Game meat 4 oz.

Fish 6 oz.

Dried fish 3 oz.

Shellfish 6 oz.

Eggs, 2 large, extra-large, or jumbo

4 oz. egg whites

Egg Beaters 6 oz.

Milk 16 oz.

Kefir 16 oz.

European buttermilk 16 oz.

Kefir cheese 6 oz.

Ricotta cheese 4 oz.

Cottage cheese 8 oz.

Tofu 12 oz.

Feta cheese 4 oz.

Goat cheese 4 oz.

Plain yogurt (Greek or regular) 8 oz., no sugar or grain

Skyr 8 oz.

Quark 8 oz.

Beans, prepared (black, kidney, roman, pinto, northern, red beans, pink beans, garbanzo beans) 8 oz.

Lentils, cooked 8 oz.

**Bacon 4 slices

**Prepared sausage (veg ok too) (no sugar): 4 oz.

**Hard and semi-hard cheese (sharp cheddar, parmesan, gouda, swiss) 2 oz.

Vegetable options (all vegetables except potatoes, sweet potatoes, peas, and corn):

- Acorn squash
- Alfalfa sprouts
- Artichoke
- Arugula/rockets
- Asparagus
- Beans (green and wax)
- Beets
- Belgian endive
- Bell pepper
- Bok choy/Chinese cabbage
- Broccoli/broccolini
- Brussels sprouts
- Butternut squash
- Cabbage
- Carrot
- Cauliflower
- Celeriac/celery root
- Celery
- Chard/silverbeet
- Chili peppers
- Cucumber
- Daikon
- Dulse
- Eggplant/aubergine
- Endive
- Escarole
- Fennel/finocchio
- Fiddlehead
- Green beans
- Garlic
- Ginger
- Green onion/scallion
- Horseradish (no sugar or seed oil)
- Jicama
- Kale
- Kimchi (no sugar or grain)
- Kohlrabi/German turnip
- Leeks
- Lettuce
- Mushrooms
- Mustard greens
- Nori
- Okra
- Onions
- Pak choi/Chinese cabbage
- Parsley
- Parsnips
- Pickles (sugar free)
- Pickled vegetables (sugar free; no olives)
- Pumpkin
- Purslane
- Rabe
- Radicchio
- Radish
- Rhubarb
- Sauerkraut (sugar free)
- Shallots
- Spinach
- Squash (all kinds)
- Tomatillo
- Tomato
- Turnips
- Water chestnut
- Watercress
- Zucchini

Condiments (add freely):

Vinegar (including balsamic)
Mustard
Salsa (2 oz. per meal)
Marinara sauce (2 oz. per meal)
Capers (2 oz. per meal)
Lemon juice
Lime juice
Cinnamon
Soy sauce
Hot sauce
Spices
Salt and pepper

Fruit (all fruit except bananas and grapes):

Apples
Apricots
Blueberries
Grapefruit
Guava
Honeydew melon
Huckleberries
Persimmon
Plums
Blackberries
Cantaloupe
Mandarin
Cranberries (fresh)
Elderberries
Figs (fresh)
Gooseberries
Kiwi
Nectarines
Orange
Papaya
Passion fruit
Peaches
Quince
Rambutan
Raspberries
Rose apple
Sapodilla
Star fruit
Strawberries
Mixed fresh fruit
Kiwi
Kumquat
Lingonberries
Lychees
Mulberries

1 Carbohydrate/starch:

Potato (4 oz. cooked)

Sweet potato or yam (4 oz. cooked)

Peas (4 oz. cooked)

Corn/corn meal (4 oz. cooked)

Rice (4 oz. cooked) (Brown better than white)

Oats (4 oz. cooked)

Quinoa (4 oz. cooked)

**1.5 oz. of bread with no sugar, additives, or preservatives (homemade, Ezekiel, 3-ingredient store-bought bread, flour tortilla, or corn tortilla)

** ¾ cup of cooked pasta

**¾ cup of Shredded Wheat (unsweetened)

**6 Triscuits or 3 rye crisp crackers or 9 Mary's Gone Crackers or 25 g three-ingredient blue corn tortilla chips (Garden of Eden, Late July)

**1.5 oz. raisins or dates or non-sweetened dried fruit

**1 banana

**1 cup grapes

Stage 2 Food Plan (Low Risk)

You may have noticed that some of the food items have two asterisks (**) next to them. These are foods that can often (but not always) be triggering for people based on research (chapter 2) and experience from providers in the field. Stage 2 offers you a food plan that is slightly less permissive (and less likely to be triggering) than the Stage 1 food plan. The only change from Stage 1 to Stage 2 is to remove any of these starred foods that seem problematic for you. For example, if hard or semi-hard cheese, bread, pasta, nut butter, bananas, grapes, bacon, prepared sausages, or anything else made with refined carbohydrates/flour (crackers) or dried fruit (raisins or dates) seem to be triggering for you, simply remove them from the above list and substitute in something else within the same macronutrient category that is less triggering. That's all!

Stage 3 Food Plan

This food plan is the least permissive and the lowest risk of the three: it is essentially a low-carb option for people who feel especially triggered by most carbohydrates (including rice, potato, oats, and such).

Breakfast:
1.5–2.5 protein
4-6 oz. berries or apple
1–3 fat

Lunch:
1.5–2.5 protein
6–12 oz. vegetable
1–3 fats

Dinner:
1.5–2.5 protein
6–12 oz. vegetable
1–3 fats

Metabolic:
0.5–1.5 protein
4–6 oz. berries or apple
1 fat

If you find fruit triggering, by all means remove the suggested fruits and substitute with vegetables. Also, beans and lentils are listed as a protein in Stage 1 and 2 plans. However, they do contain carbohydrates, and if you are on the Stage 3 plan, you may choose to replace beans and lentils with some of the other protein sources if you continue to have cravings while eating legumes.

People who choose a Stage 3 plan may decide to reintroduce some low-risk carbohydrates after they feel stabilized. If you are one of these people, by all means, do so! I would love for every one of you to have the most permissive and abundant food plan that you can. However, know that with reintroduction, cravings can come back, and you might be triggered. Therefore, it's ideal to have support in place during reintroduction processes, and to proceed only after having integrated some skills into your recovery (from chapters 10–12). If your cravings have significantly reduced after the first thirty days of adhering to your food plan and you are feeling courageous, add back one of the below to one of your meals (of your choosing).

Starch options (after first thirty days):

Other fruits (6 oz.) one at a time from the list of fruits

Potato (4 oz. cooked)

Sweet potato or yam (4 oz. cooked)

Rice (4 oz. cooked)

Quinoa (4 oz. cooked)

If that add-in works well after seven days, then you are welcome to try to add in another item. If it doesn't work well and if cravings get worse, then you will know that for now this is a trigger food and that it would be wise to remove it again from your food plan.

Here are some things to keep in mind as you implement your food plan. If you make personal adjustments, make sure to do so according to the three key principles of a food plan. Also, if you start a food plan, but are hungry/losing weight at a rate of more than 1 pound a week, increase the protein, fat, and veggies by 25 percent per week. Also try to target a total daily intake of 1 gram of protein per kilogram of your body weight. If you exercise regularly, you can edge toward the higher end of ranges, especially on the days you exercise. Don't hesitate to see a nutritionist or dietitian for personalized adjustments either. In the "Important Links" section of the Resources List at http://www.newharbinger.com/54681, I provide a link to Amy Reichelt's website, where you will find some recipes; there's also a handout of solution-focused questions to help you with making adjustments to your plan.

Don't let yourself get too hungry! If you need to adjust up, do so starting with veggies and protein, then fat, then carbs, keeping ratios generally similar. If you want to break your breakfast into two meals, because you are not hungry at 7 a.m. but get very hungry at 11, by all means, have half at 7 a.m. and the other half at 11 a.m.

Sometimes, cravings and hunger can be difficult to parse. If you feel hungry, it might be that you are having a craving. If you're craving, it might just be that you're hungry. If you're hungry or experiencing cravings and worried that you are on the path toward bingeing, try this: eat 4 oz. of a lean protein like cooked tofu, chicken, pork, or fish. Wait fifteen minutes. If you still feel hungry or are experiencing cravings, it's likely that you're not truly hungry and just craving, and should deploy some craving management skills (chapter 10). If the protein consumption killed the craving or hunger, it could be that you were simply hungry, and you may need to think about increasing the quantities of food you are eating on your daily food plan.

Do you have to do the food plans perfectly? NO! See chapter 9 for information about harm reduction. These are guidelines, not hard-and-fast rules. The most important principle is variety, eating enough, and getting rid of as much of the junk as you can.

Can you keep drinking alcohol? I think that will be up to you. If you misuse alcohol or have an alcohol use disorder, certainly take care of that first with professional help. If you have a drink every once in a while—once a month, say—and you feel it doesn't affect your cravings, it might be alright to keep it in your food plan. However, remember that alcohol activates the same reward circuitry, that intoxication will adversely affect your mood and impulse control, and that cross addiction or addiction transfer could occur (Wilcox 2021). I'd say that the safest course would be to let go of alcohol at the same time you let go of sugar and ultra-processed foods to maximize your chance of success.

If you're a person with medical problems related to your weight and want to lose weight, but haven't while on these food plans, don't lose hope. After three to six months of stabilization, and once you've got a good support system in place, consider slowly and steadily decreasing your portion sizes by no more than 10 percent per month and watch for resurgence in your cravings and obsessions. If they come back, you might not be quite ready yet. It's fine. This is a lifelong process.

Parting Thoughts

There are many more starter food plans out there to choose from. Vera Tarman's excellent book *Food Junkies* lists several options (Tarman 2019). The various food addiction treatment programs in the "Accessing Professional Help" bonus chapter at http://www.newharbinger.com/54681

have their own recommended food plans, too. I do caution against adopting food plans targeting weight loss, for now.

Notably, our biology and food preferences shift over time, as do our cravings. As this occurs, we need to adapt our food plan and overall treatment approach accordingly. In the past, it was all about undercooked chocolate chip cookies for me (dripping and melty, on top of vanilla ice cream with walnuts). Then when I finally let those go completely—over ten years ago now—it became all about sourdough toast with butter. My cravings changed. My obsessions changed.

Honoring these variations in our cravings is important as we consider what to eat more of and what to avoid. Sometimes, the thing that's undermining our progress is overexposure to a food cue that we haven't quite yet identified—perhaps our child brought home Girl Scout cookies, and their colorful boxes are triggering cravings. At other times, it might be our mood has shifted, or an imbalance in another lifestyle factor needs to be addressed (chapters 10–12).

Fad Diets

Recall that Sara (chapter 6) found some relief from cravings via low-carb diets (Atkins, keto, South Beach, Whole 30). Whenever she adhered to them, her cravings went away and she lost weight. But the longest she lasted was six weeks on these; the carbs would slowly move back in. Although low-carb approaches are often easier for people with food addiction than other diets, because the cravings dissipate, for Sara, it wasn't enough. Perhaps these diets were too restrictive *for her*. Perhaps she was still eating particular foods that she hadn't considered as being possibly triggering for her. Perhaps she didn't have enough support. Most importantly, those nutritional plans were only telling her the *what* (eat this way), not the *how* (all the tools you're learning in this book), and it wasn't sustainable.

David Katz calls fad diets "a nefarious industry," and ineffective. "The problem is that fools and fanatics are so sure and wise people full of doubt," he says, paraphrasing Bertrand Russell. Fad diets, usually touted by someone who claims to be the "messiah of nutrition," "promise the moon and stars" and guarantee "effortless and instantaneous" solutions. If fad diets are at all effective, he asks, "Then where are all the thin people then…since these fad diets have been around for decades?" As a culture, he says, "We've been living on a diet of diets and we are getting fatter…it's not working" (Katz 2023).

I agree that fad diets in general should be approached with skepticism. Studies in the general population show that all diets—whether fads or doctor-recommended low-carb/low fat/calorie reduction-based diets—seem to result in similar amounts of weight loss (usually modest on the whole). But most people cannot sustain the loss for any significant period of time using these approaches (Wilcox 2021).

Remember how 20 percent of people in the general population meet criteria for food addiction according to the YFAS? I would suggest that many of the people who don't lose weight in these studies have food addiction that is not being considered. Fad diets fail to consider that the brain needs to be rewired and ask people to employ impossible amounts of willpower. They fail to acknowledge the importance of abstaining from certain foods that sensitize our reward system. They are often excessively restrictive, causing hunger and nutrient deficiency, which fuels addiction. They don't consider the needs of the individual, and they often include multiple ultra-processed food options, like keto bars or bombs and sugar replacement sweeteners.

That said, the fad diets that are the closest to the plans offered in this book—Mediterranean, keto, Atkins, paleo—encourage increased consumption of nutrient-dense, high-protein, high-fiber foods and/or avoidance of refined and other carbohydrates, and may benefit your physical and mental health. Because they have been more widely studied, we offer this information below as good reason to believe that adopting the kind of plan offered in this book will confer similar benefits for you, regardless of whether weight loss occurs.

Studies show that diets high in protein and whole foods but low in sugar and refined carbohydrates reduce the risk of and can reverse insulin resistance, high blood pressure, hypertriglyceridemia, metabolic syndrome, cardiovascular disease, diabetes, and premature death. They can also reduce the risk of cancer, improve renal function, reduce inflammation, decrease chronic pain, reverse polycystic ovarian disease, and improve pancreatic function (Lustig 2021; Unwin 2021a; Bikman 2022; Westman 2021; Nilson et al. 2022; Nilson et al. 2023; Wilcox 2021; Gomes Goncalves et al. 2023). A food addiction-like diet can have other mental health effects that extend beyond their effects on addiction circuitry, improving cognitive function and attentional capacity and reducing Alzheimer's risk, depression, mood swings, anxiety, ADHD symptoms, and aggression (Taubes 2021; Vora 2022; Kaplan 2023; Reichelt 2023; Brown 2022; Avena 2021; Bayes, Schloss, and Sibbritt 2022; Opie et al. 2018; Staudacher et al. 2024). Weight release can improve numerous other health problems, including reduction of diabetes and heart disease risk, reduction of insulin resistance, and improvement of osteoarthritis, obstructive sleep apnea, GERD, acne, and psoriasis (Wilcox 2021).

The Food Plan Is Just the First Step

This is a big change. It's not just about the food plan. It's not just whole foods but the *whole you* that's important. This means considering not just your physical symptoms but also the mental, emotional, and even spiritual aspects of your well-being. Nutritional changes are key to rewiring your brain, but the rest of it is also essential to help you make and maintain what can initially feel like a drastic, impossible, countercultural shift in behavior and habits. Please do not just read this chapter and be done—so many of us food addiction types have a tendency to cut and run after we get the food plan. Read chapters 9–12 just as closely, as the majority of us need much more than some information about what to eat.

CHAPTER 9

How to Eat: Abstinence versus Harm Reduction

"I had to be rigid to get free, but I didn't get free to spend the rest of my life being rigid. I want to be more like water and less like rocks...I just want inner peace."

—David Wiss, *Food Junkies Podcast*

You've identified your starter food plan, and you're ready to go. But you aren't clear on how truly black and white you need to be about all this. In this chapter, I'll help you decide.

Some people flourish when they embark upon a stringent, *abstinence-based* approach—drawing clear lines around what they eat and don't eat, then staying within defined boundaries. Clear lines give us freedom from having to make lots of choices. However, speaking from experience, most of us with food addiction do better in the long run with a less rigid approach—with fuzzier boundaries, less black and white. Such an approach is also called a *harm reduction* approach and is commonly used in place of an abstinence model in the addiction treatment world.

In this chapter, I will present the pros and cons of both approaches. Your circumstances and personality may make one a better fit for you than another. It's important for you to know what the risks and benefits of each are. You might even decide to embrace aspects of both approaches when you're done reading, like I have (more on that later).

Pros and Cons of an Abstinence-Based Approach

In traditional addiction treatment, people are encouraged to completely abstain from the problem substance. This is the approach embraced by the 12-step community. For many people, quitting the substance completely is what is required to break free from the obsessions and cravings.

It's clear what abstinence means for substances of abuse: just don't use it. With food addiction, the definition of abstinence is less clear, and can vary. It can range from "no sugar, no flour," "eat 100 percent within my food plan," "no ultra-processed foods," or "no slider foods" (foods that are calorie-dense and fast-acting). For some of us, clear rules like these are what we need to turn off the obsession. One benefit: the "just one bite" justification has no room in an abstinence-based plan.

Personally, I felt like giving up sugar was a quantum shift—the effects on my cravings and bingeing were immediate and profound. Ellen Vora says about her own recovery that "abstaining from the drug-like foods [was what changed everything] and was the crucial off ramp" from problem eating for her, after which she started to have normalized eating and re-experience satiety (Vora 2022). For Vera Tarman, it was the ticket to freedom, too, and her book *Food Junkies* gives some wonderful ideas on how to approach recovery in this way (Tarman 2019).

Abstinence solves several problems from a neurochemical and psychological perspective. The primary pro of an abstinence-based model is that it restores brain function more quickly in desired ways. We know from behavioral neuroscience and experimental psychology that removal of a reward or outcome extinguishes the habitual behavior, and cues associated with use lose their power to drive a response. For many people with addictions, though, even after prolonged abstinence, just a little taste can reignite the brain's reward signals and turn on the behavior once again (Guyenet 2022a, 2022b). The addiction circuit that had been extinguished is reactivated, and the food reward-seeking behavior takes over once again. In an abstinence-based approach, we avoid the trigger foods completely to stay safe.

Second, abstinence helps the prefrontal cortex heal and improves global impulse control. The less we expose our brains to the ultra-processed substances that damage our neurons, the more we improve our decision making abilities. With abstinence, wiser decisions rise to the top, and like exercising a muscle, our brain becomes more adept at making the right choices in the face of temptation. Clear boundaries take away some of the decision fatigue and internalized negotiations so many of us struggle with, alleviating some of the cognitive demands upon our embattled prefrontal cortices, giving us freedom from having to make hard choices.

Third, abstinence restores our emotional health. Recall that many of these addictive substances, including highly rewarding food, cause depression and anxiety through tolerance and withdrawal. When it's out of our system, these physiological changes begin to reverse within weeks (Wilcox 2021).

The cons of an abstinence-based approach for food addiction, however, need to be acknowledged. First, the truth about humans: we rebel against rules, especially if they come from outside ourselves, but we also rebel against ourselves and our own rules, too. Excess rigidity can give us the urge to revolt and do the opposite, and this is especially a problem for those of us with comorbid eating disorder tendencies (as we discussed in chapter 6). David Unwin and Clarissa of *Food Junkies* observe in their practices that people rev up in anticipation of quitting an addictive substance or making a big change in their eating (Unwin 2021a). I struggled with the night-before-ramp-up with food, too. "I'll get back on the plan tomorrow. Tonight, I'll eat whatever I want," was a common refrain. This would almost always result in a binge. The more rigid we are with ourselves, the more our brain begins to hyper-value these "forbidden foods" until we snap and fall prey to our more maladaptive urges.

A second problem with being too rigid is that getting into recovery and staying in recovery is more challenging for food than other substances. We need to eat to live, and as Ellen Vora says, "We have to open up that cage minimum three times a day and interact with that tiger" (Vora 2022). We should prepare ourselves for some struggle instead of expecting perfection out of the gate because it's more realistic. The ubiquitous presence of ultra-processed, high-sugar foods means it often takes a lot of work, learning, community building, and time for us to fully let them go, made worse by the discomfort of withdrawal dysphoria. By expecting some challenges, we can prevent ourselves from feeling demoralized, building community with others to keep us from isolating ourselves. Some people need to take it slower than others, and there's no judgment around that. An abstinence approach doesn't provide the flexibility needed to adapt to a food-centric environment.

A third problem is that individuals differ in their food sensitivities, environments, and lifestyles, all of which can influence optimal food plans. It will take time and experimentation to find out what your personal trigger foods are.

Finally, abstinence approaches can feel shaming and exclusionary, further fueling problematic perfectionistic and self-critical thinking. Kathleen DesMaisons, author of *Potatoes not Prozac*, said on *Food Junkies* that she feels the word abstinence is "grim" and creates a feeling of deprivation and that people can feel "beaten up by the word" (2022).

Twelve-step meetings for food addiction recovery like OA, Food Addicts Anonymous (FAA), and GreySheet are free and easy to access. But some of the subgroups have stricter, one-size-fits-all food plans and hard-and-fast rules about quantities weighing and measuring (FAA, GreySheet), which can fuel unhelpful cycles of perfectionism and shame. Some 12-step food groups don't even let you talk until you are sober in meetings—a time when you need the support the most. That said, there are also OA meetings that do not require anyone to follow a one-size-fits-all food plan. To find a meeting for you, you may need to shop around.

Timothy Brewerton, psychiatrist and editor of *Eating Disorders, Addictions, and Substance Use Disorders*, reminds us that we still have very little research in food addiction treatment and "It's not clear to what extent abstinence is required" (Brewerton 2022). Just because some people find freedom through this mechanism doesn't mean it will work for all people with food addiction. Why should you force yourself to be completely abstinent if we don't yet even know what works best?

David Wiss states that real life requires flexibility around food. Although he loves the steps, spirituality, and social support aspects of 12-step meetings, he isn't a fan of the defeating messaging that is present in some of the groups, like that you have to start from day one "if you have an extra ounce of protein." It doesn't make sense to be so precise when nature is NOT super precise—whether it's 4 oz. or 5 oz. is irrelevant when it comes to a piece of fish, since no fish is identical (Wiss 2023). I completely agree.

In sum, an abstinence-based approach has some great advantages, but for many (probably most) of us, when it comes to food, a harm reduction approach is a better fit.

Harm Reduction

A harm reduction approach—which is about safe or managed use of an addictive substance, rather than complete abstinence from it—is the other way to go. Harm reduction is an addiction treatment philosophy that is focused on minimizing the negative consequences of use without necessarily requiring the activity to stop completely. It is also an evidence-based approach and widely utilized in substance use disorder treatment.

Harm reduction models focus on minimizing death, injury, and morbidity over abstinence, embracing the strategies of managed use, safer use, and managing comorbid conditions concurrent to addressing the addiction. Counselors treating patients in these harm reduction models are encouraged to respect the client's right to make informed choices as well as their capacity to make change. It conceptualizes people as individuals living on a spectrum rather than imposing a rigid one-size-fits-all treatment model.

Here are some examples of harm reduction approaches in substance use disorder treatment: continuing to allow someone to stay in a treatment center to work on their addiction to methamphetamine and alcohol (even though they still smoke marijuana regularly), needle exchange programs, and opioid replacement therapy with methadone and suboxone for opioid use disorder. The end goal of harm reduction, in many cases, is abstinence; it's just a different way of getting there.

You may not feel drawn to this harm-reduction idea for yourself because you just want to be told what to do and then do it. It seems so much easier. You believe that if you just relinquish control to some rule, you will finally get free. But haven't you tried that before and gotten stuck, over and over? Haven't you rebelled?

Harm reduction approaches move us away from militant one-sized-fits-all restriction that triggers rebound binge eating, providing the tools to make intentional and self-compassionate choices and to live in a more empowered and self-determined way!

Here are some examples of how you can use a harm reduction approach in your recovery from food addiction.

You can try keeping certain higher-risk foods in your food plan, but limit your intake of them to certain settings or situations. Ann Saffi Biasetti, therapist and author of *Befriending Your Body*, says one of her clients finds she can eat sugar when "in relationship with" others (such as getting ice cream with her young daughter), whereas her mind is much more activated and she struggles more around sugar when alone (Biasetti 2022). Similarly, I can eat bread and butter in restaurants, but I really struggle eating this combination in moderation when I'm at home, so I don't…at home. Being alone at home increases my risk, which is why I implement my most stringent boundaries and controls in that setting. From a neurobiological perspective, environment-based boundaries make sense: our brains are more sensitive to addictive cues in locations we typically associate with addictive behavior.

Another example of a harm reduction approach involves stepping down, rather than abstaining all at once, from highly rewarding foods. When I stopped eating sugar, I did continue to use maple syrup, home-made raisin or date paste, and all-fruit jelly as sweeteners to reduce feelings of deprivation occasionally (a few times a month) at home. I did that for many years after stopping sugar, using them rarely and in moderation. However, when the COVID-19 pandemic hit, I became very adept at baking treats at home with these "safe" sweeteners that tasted just like store-bought desserts, and I lost control of my eating again. While I never went back to regular store-made baked goods, I did overeat these home-baked treats for a while. Ultimately, I had to completely stop them, too. Now, I feel sane around food again and have adjusted my boundaries. You will find where you need to draw the line for yourself, too, but it's not the same for everyone.

A third example of how to apply harm reduction to your eating relates to your implementation of your food plan. Say you're on the Stage 1 food plan: is it alright to have piece of quiche or a scoop of or lasagna even though you haven't measured how much protein versus fat versus carbohydrate is in it, especially if you're out at a restaurant or with family? Sure it is, if you're embracing a harm reduction approach! Just do a bit of an estimate in your head to make it match your food plan as much as possible. For example, if I order pasta at a restaurant, to make sure to get my nutrients, I'll also get a side of salmon and a big salad, with dressing on the side. I'll eat all the salmon and salad, and only 1/3 of the pasta, taking the rest home. It's an estimate, but close.

- *John's Story*

    John, 42, was recently diagnosed with type 2 diabetes and gluten intolerance. Now, he faces the challenge of adhering to strict dietary requirements to manage his conditions. Although he doesn't eat most baked goods, sweets, or flour-containing items, he still eats a protein bar as a dessert in the evening with alternative sweeteners in it. He also uses Carbonaut or Ezekiel bread for his sandwiches, enjoys Halo Top ice cream when his family is eating real ice cream, and eats cauliflower crust pizza and some almond flour baked goods. By focusing on small, sustainable changes and utilizing the support network around him, John has reclaimed control over his eating habits and health, without sacrificing certain eating experiences that feel rich to him.

Molly, Clarissa, and many of their podcast guests advocate for a harm reduction approach, often emphasizing "harm reduction with an end goal of abstinence." In his practice, David Wiss supports people who want to do a slower transition off of sugar and ultra-processed foods using a stepwise approach that is personalized to their lifestyles and needs (Wiss 2023). Ellen Vora advocates for an attitude of "ease and loose grip," to avoid activating the scarcity mindset (Vora 2022).

Not everyone is a fan of using harm reduction in food addiction treatment, though: there are cons. Abstinence proponents worry about missing opportunities to move people forward, voicing concerns that people just won't get well without true abstinence. For some people, black-and-white limit-setting feels comforting and is simpler and clearer. David Wiss says,

"Some people need boxes" (Wiss 2023). As we've discussed, an abstinence-based approach is indeed probably safest from a neurobiological perspective since it minimizes opportunities for the reinstatement of behaviors; when we do re-expose ourselves to trigger food, it has the potential to open the cage and let the beast out again.

Relapse and Food Addiction

Because it's harder to define abstinence with food than it is with other substances, the term "relapse" is of questionable utility in regards to food addiction. With 12-step approaches to recovery from addiction, people often count days and celebrate sobriety anniversaries; with food, the specific sobriety date is usually less obvious. Within the context of food addiction, I personally think the word "relapse" is not useful, and I encourage you to relinquish it. Better terms are "return to use" when you go back to eating a particular food item that was once off your food plan, and "recurrence of symptoms" when food addiction symptoms come back.

Susan Peirce Thompson said on *Food Junkies* that over time, as she's experienced her own slipups and reframed them as slips not relapse, she's realized that part of recovery is letting go of "unflinching perfectionism." She currently believes that "it's only helpful to start at day one if your whole program needs to be demolished and built again from the ground up" (Thompson 2022). Her second book, *Rezoom*, was inspired by these personal experiences, and it has a softer, more nuanced message for her readers than her first.

Ann Saffi Biasetti says she doesn't use the word "relapse" because it's both "harsh" and "binary." Instead, she uses the word "relearning" when someone slips because struggle is an opportunity to learn a new skill (Biasetti 2022).

Regardless of what we call it, the fact is that those of us in recovery from food addiction are always at risk of slipping back into our old ways, whether through a binge or in a more insidious fashion. You'll learn skills for how to come back from a slip in chapters 10–12. Clarissa and Molly of *Food Junkies* say that in their experience, for clients with food addiction who return to use and find themselves spiraling, it can take from three days to a few weeks to get stabilized and craving-free when they stop again, depending on the length and intensity of their use during the spiral.

Recovery as a Continuum Over Time

Remember, your recovery from food addiction will be far from perfect. Most recovery trajectories are in no way linear, and I've never met someone with a recovery that happened overnight. Recovery is a continuum. John Kelly's recovery research has found that it takes many people about 7–8 years and multiple interventions before they get one year of abstinence from alcohol or other substances, but that their abstinence periods and qualities of life keep improving over these first years, too. We need to allow ourselves to practice recovery! "Just keep trying," he says, because chances are you'll eventually get well (Kelly 2024).

David Wiss says many people need more structure in the beginning, and start out with a 12-step approach, but need less and less rigidity the more time they are in recovery. Similarly, regarding weighing and measuring, he says it "can be a good tool in the early stages but I'm not convinced that spending your life weighing and measuring food is the jam. It can't be (Wiss 2023)." Lifelong weighing and measuring also doesn't let you learn to honor your hunger and fullness cues as they come back online with recovery.

Does this mean you can look forward to actually eating a cookie now and again after you've been abstinent and stable for a long time (years)? We don't know. For people in recovery from alcohol use disorder who go back to drinking alcohol after decades sober, some are able to drink in moderation, but others spiral quickly back into a use disorder; those who have a more severe illness are more likely to do poorly with attempts at reintroduction, studies show (Kelly 2024).

Personally, I have no desire at all to go back to eating cookies someday, now that they are out of my system. I see no reason to rock the boat or fix what isn't broken, now that I no longer have to fight insatiable cravings.

The Right Path for You

Ultimately, here are the keys to keep in mind when determining the right path for you.

1. If your eating deteriorates every time you tell yourself that you can't have flour (for example), or you're someone that has a huge binge and says, "I'll start tomorrow" frequently, you may do better with harm reduction.

2. If you have an eating disorder history, or tendencies toward it (see chapter 6), lean toward harm reduction.

3. If you tend toward perfectionism, you may do better with harm reduction (Clarissa's wisdom).

4. If your lifestyle is such that an abstinence-based approach or adhering to one of the food plans is not feasible (e.g. night-shift work), having more flexibility in your food plan might work best for you.

5. If you tend to get triggered every time you have a little taste of a particular food item and find it makes you go off the rails, then it might be important to be abstinent around that food item.

6. Sometimes, the people with more severe food addiction (i.e., higher scores on the YFAS) also need more structure, especially at first, and may need a more abstinence-based approach to start and/or for a lifetime.

7. Sometimes, people in early (first 4 weeks) or mid-recovery (4 weeks–1 year) need more of an abstinence-based approach that can be reduced with time (slowly, and probably not all the way back to eating your most triggering, highly rewarding foods).

8. You are welcome to use elements of both, like I do!

For a list of solution-focused questions to help you discern which model suits you best, visit http://www.newharbinger.com/54681.

CHAPTER 10

Skills to Reduce Food Cue Sensitivity

"If it's in the house, it's in your mouth."

—Clarissa Kennedy, *Food Junkies Podcast*

Hopefully, it's clear to you by now how reducing sugar and ultra-processed food while increasing fresh, whole foods will reduce your cue sensitivity, improve your impulse control and mood, and reduce cravings so that you can regain sanity and peace around food and eating. Changing what and how you eat is the foundation of the recovery puzzle.

If you're like many of us, you've tried to change your eating habits, but it hasn't stuck. I've been there—I used to joke I was a quitting expert because I'd quit smoking hundreds of times, just like I've started and stopped countless food plans. For those with food addiction, good intentions often aren't enough. As Michael Moss says, "Addictions steal our free will" (Moss 2021).

Changing an addictive habit is hard, so you'll need extra skills and strategies. The next three chapters will cover tools to help you stay on track and positively impact your addictive brain chemistry, speeding up your progress. These will both help you stick with your intentions long enough to reap the rewards and have direct beneficial effects on your reward-seeking brain circuitry.

Addictive behavior stems from three core brain issues: heightened sensitivity to food cues, poor stress/emotion regulation, and impaired impulse control. In chapter 10, you'll learn how to guard against food-cue sensitivity. Chapter 11 covers skills for managing stress and emotions, and chapter 12 focuses on improving impulse control and decision making.

The Food Cue Sensitivity Problem

When I open a can of tuna or kitty food, our cat comes running, driven by the sound or smell—an example of food cue sensitivity. Like pets, we're wired to respond to environmental cues, and today's world is flooded with them. Clarissa found 160 food cues in a single day (Lembke 2021a, 2021b). The smell of cookies, a glimpse of a donut, or a taste of ice cream can light up our reward centers instantly. How do we protect ourselves from this barrage? How do we keep our reward-seeking brains from derailing us? How can we ease up on the accelerator?

Avoid Getting Triggered

One great way to protect yourself from getting derailed by environmental cues is to prevent cravings from getting triggered in the first place. Proactive solutions will give you more bang for your buck. This is because once your reward circuits have been flared up and a craving takes hold, it can be very difficult and uncomfortable to resist.

To do so, you can change your environment. First, identify the triggers in your environment you are most sensitive to. Next, work to remove them. Doing this to the best of your ability is especially important in early recovery.

Triggers can take many forms: the foods themselves, or related sights, sounds, smells, or images in ads. Places like stores, restaurants, and work break rooms where you've indulged before, or people you tend to overeat with, can also derail your recovery. Social gatherings, parties, and holidays combine food cues and social pressure, making them especially tough.

Even certain tastes or hidden sugars in your food plan might trigger cravings. Do you find that whenever you eat a particular item, you find that within a certain period of time—either instantly, or even a few hours later—you start to crave highly rewarding foods? Check your cabinets for foods that consistently seem to lead to cravings, and double check their labels for one of the 262 kinds of sugars.

Sometimes, you may be conscious of being triggered in the moment, but many times, you won't be. You may suddenly discover you are in the midst of an intense craving or already in the midst of a binge without knowing how you got there. Trying to identify the hidden trigger by looking backwards might work, but it also might not. So recognize that this will be a process, and that awareness of your personal triggers will not happen overnight.

Exercise: **Rating Cravings**

For a week, I invite you to do some note-taking. Take seven pieces of paper (one for each day of the week) and create five columns on each. The leftmost column will be used to mark the hours of the day while you're awake. The next one over you will use to rate your cravings (on a scale of 1–5). Rate your craving at a set time four times a day, every four hours. Also in this column, mark moments during the day when your cravings are notably high or when you engage in a problematic food behavior. In the third column, write down what you eat throughout the day (quantities and content). In the fourth column, describe who you were with and what you were doing throughout the day. In the fifth column, jot down important observations about mood, sleep, activity, hunger levels, environmental food exposures, and so forth. After the week is up, review your notes and see if they give you more insight into what some of your own personal sensitivities might be.

Exercise: **Journaling on Roadblocks**

Journal about the following question for five minutes. When you've tried to change your eating habits in the past, what was happening around and within you (emotions and thoughts) around the time that you "gave up"?

Exercise: **Personal Triggers**

Consider this list of my own personal triggers:

- Seeing a loaf of fresh bread on the counter, when I wasn't expecting it
- The Trader Joe's freezer aisle or the area in Whole Foods where I used to buy cookie dough
- The smell of baked goods, especially sweets
- Parties
- Family gatherings
- Being tired or overwhelmed and alone in the house when high-risk food items are present
- Having a high-flour, high-carbohydrate meal without adequate protein or fiber

Now, for five minutes, brainstorm a list of your own personal environmental food cue triggers.

Now that you've identified some of the things in your environment that light up your reward centers and veer you off course most, work toward reducing your exposure to them.

First, get your problem foods out of the house. Ask your family if they would be willing to change their eating habits, especially when you're first starting. Start shopping at different grocery stores (to avoid the food aisle where the cookie dough is stored). Take a different driving route on your way home from work (to avoid a favorite fast-food restaurant). Avoid the break room at work.

Always have an "escape plan" from high-risk social gatherings, like parties. Always have a pre-planned excuse for leaving early if you're finding yourself getting triggered, like "I'm not feeling well," and "I'm sorry, but I have to go home." Practice making the excuse—saying it out loud with a recovery buddy or family member in the know—before you go. And always have a pre-thought-out plan for how you'll escape, transportation-wise, even if it means driving separately from your spouse or calling a Lyft.

If your cravings occur consistently at a certain time of day, or minutes after you eat a particular meal, consider that there may be a hidden item in your food plan that is triggering you. Switch up the brand of salsa that you've been using to one that doesn't have any sugar in it at all for thirty days, to see what happens. Take out the flour tortilla you eat every day at lunch that you'd been wondering about but holding onto, and see how it goes—recall that, for some people, flour can often be a trigger food; some consider it as bad as sugar. Consider seeing a nutritionist and learn more about how to read food labels or refine your food plan to make it less triggering.

Exercise: Action Plan

Write down three things that you can do this week to decrease your food cue exposure.

Physical Activity

One of my favorite ways to choke out an addiction is through physical exercise. It's simple and it works. Studies show that walking, hiking, yoga, running, tennis, climbing, or swimming all help reduce addictive behavior.

Specific to this chapter's focus, physical activity reduces "cue-induced reactivity" in the brain's reward areas, including to cues for rewarding food (Wilcox 2021; Dera et al. 2023). Even moderate exercise, like ten minutes of cycling, can lower brain reactivity to cues, as a study in smokers showed (Van Rensburg, Taylor, and Hodgson 2009).

Don't stress about which exercise is best for your addictive brain wiring. Instead, find what brings you joy and fits your lifestyle, then gradually increase intensity and frequency over time (Wilcox 2021).

Avoid thinking of exercise as a way to burn calories. It can become compulsive when focused on weight loss. Plus, the more you exercise, the hungrier you get—fueling addiction circuits, as you know. Adjust food intake to match exercise with guidance from your nutritionist to avoid hunger.

Sleep

Protecting our brains from food triggers also depends on getting enough sleep. Studies show that sleep deprivation and irregular sleep patterns increase binge eating and weight gain.

Sleep deprivation increases ghrelin, lowers leptin, and boosts appetite, making us more sensitive to food cues (Samakidou et al. 2023). Orexin, a neurohormone related to sleep and arousal, may drive these effects, and medications targeting orexin are being developed to address sleep issues, addiction, and binge eating (Mehr et al. 2021).

Specific to this chapter's focus, lack of sleep enhances the brain's sensitivity to food cues, making reward centers hyperresponsive (Samakidou et al. 2023; Wilcox 2021; Katsunuma et al. 2017). Getting enough sleep helps protect us.

Adults aged 18–60 should aim for at least 7 hours of sleep (Samakidou et al. 2023). Napping to catch up on sleep can improve mood and reduce hedonic eating (Motomura, Katsunuma, et al. 2017; Motomura, Kitamura, et al. 2017). However, night shifts and irregular sleep patterns pose their own challenges.

If insomnia prevents you from getting enough rest, start with sleep hygiene. One study found that sleep hygiene counseling reduced calorie intake by 250 kcal in overweight adults (Tasali et al. 2022; Samakidou et al. 2023). Avoid non-sleep activities in bed (like working on your computer and watching television), minimize screen exposure, and ensure your bedroom is dark and quiet.

If self-help approaches don't work, consider professional help for insomnia, such as cognitive behavior therapy for insomnia (CBT-I), which is a highly effective therapy specifically for sleep issues (Trauer et al. 2015). Melatonin may also be an option if deemed safe by your healthcare provider.

Honor Your Own Biorhythms

Another key way to protect your brain and recovery from derailment is to honor your own biorhythms. The acronym HALTTSS (from AA and Sweet

Sobriety) stands for Hungry, Angry, Lonely, Tired, Thirsty, Sick, and Stressed. These are states of mind that activate addictive circuits and fuel addictive behaviors. Times when you should honor your own needs include mealtime (protect yourself from getting hungry), hydration time (keep water with you, and try not to get thirsty) and nap or bedtime (protect yourself from fatigue and overwhelm). The better you can take care of yourself in these areas, the more resilient to food cues you will be.

What does this mean in practice? In many cases, this means going against the grain. For one, some of us find that the food plan that most supports our recovery doesn't align with what others around us expect from us. For example, in my family growing up, it was typical to eat a small breakfast, maybe eat a small lunch or skip it, and then have a large dinner around 7 p.m. I've learned with my recovery that I do best with an entirely different schedule: my largest meal is often breakfast, I do best with four medium-sized meals throughout the day, and I eat my dinner early, at 4:30 or 5 p.m. My partner likes a larger later dinner, so we often don't eat meals together: we connect during other times of the day and week.

My countercultural eating habits raise people's eyebrows: I eat tons of veggies and will eat whole cucumbers, peppers, or tomatoes, or a big bin of fresh kale in the middle of a meeting or on long car ride with friends because it makes me feel good and it nourishes my body. I'll also often bring pre-cooked tofu cubes with me to a restaurant to add them to my meal so I have enough protein. The more I care for myself, the less likely it is I will feel deprived at the end of the meal when someone at my table bites into their apple pie á la mode dessert. I love a short midday nap—it energizes and restores me—and I've arranged my schedule to accommodate that most days of the week. By keeping myself nourished and rested when my body needs it most, I'm protecting my brain from food cues and promoting my recovery.

Many of us with food addiction are notorious people pleasers. Therefore, it can be especially hard for people with food addiction to honor our own biorhythms and prioritize them over the expectations and desires of other people. But as a recovering people pleaser myself, I know that if I have learned how to do it, you can too. Whenever you can, eat, exercise, drink, and sleep when your body needs it—not when you're "supposed to."

Also, it's normal in early recovery to be unsure of your body's needs. If you're not yet sure what your requirements are for sleep or other necessities, start with four good-sized meals a day and at least eight hours a night of sleep. The longer you are in recovery, the more awareness you will have about what variations suit you best and how to maintain stability in your brain's reward circuitry. When you do know, honor it. Instead of conforming to the world's expectations for you, put your needs first. The more you take care of yourself, the more resilient to food cue exposure your brain will be.

Practice Mindfulness

Mindfulness is a mental state in which we are aware of the present moment. Being more mindful will help your addicted brain heal in a variety of ways, studies show (Bowen et al. 2021; Bowen et al. 2014).

It's particularly helpful is in managing sensitivity to environmental cues. One study found that an app-based mindfulness intervention reduced the responses of the brain's reward network to both smoking cues and smoking behavior in chronic smokers (Janes et al. 2019). The more mindful you are of your personal environmental triggers, the easier it will be to problem-solve around how to avoid them. Avoiding them will give your brain time to heal, peacefully.

A regular meditation practice is one way you can build your mindfulness muscle. The more you intentionally practice, the more attentive you will be, naturally, when a craving or unwanted food behavior gets triggered, and the more you'll understand yourself and your personal vulnerabilities.

Exercise: **Basic Mindfulness Meditation**

For one week, meditate for a short time every morning. Set a timer for ten minutes, sit upright in a comfortable position, and close your eyes. Allow yourself to breathe naturally and observe the sensations of your breath in your nostrils, chest, or belly. You might choose a particular spot of the body on which to focus. At some point, your mind will wander, which is normal. When you have realized your attention has drifted from your breath, and that you are lost in thought, plans, or worries, just notice that you are thinking, and gently return your attention back to the physical sensations of your breath. Observe and accept what is happening, without judgment. Notice the sensations of breathing and the natural tendency toward distraction with an equal amount of neutrality. Continue to nudge yourself back to the breath when you are aware your mind has drifted. When the timer goes off, thank yourself, and when you feel ready, open your eyes.

When a Craving Hits

Unfortunately, no matter how hard we try to protect ourselves, food cue exposures and cravings happen; we can't prevent them all. Thankfully, there are some effective skills and solutions to deploy in those moments to decrease the chance that you will act on your cravings when they come up.

What exactly is a craving? In brief, it is an urge to use, and it can manifest physically (elevated heart rate, muscle stiffness, shortness of breath, feelings of hunger), emotionally (anger, irritability, panic, depression) and pre-behaviorally (euphoric recall, obsessive thinking, fantasizing).

The first key principle of craving management is: don't feed it. The less we act on our cravings, as hard as it can be, the more quickly our brains will heal, and the faster the problematic conditioned memories you learned about in chapter 3 will be extinguished. With time, often within minutes, a craving will certainly pass.

What can you do instead?

Get Busy

First, take action to manage a craving. Try going for a walk, calling a friend, engaging in a hobby, going shopping (but not for food), catching up on work emails, hitting the gym, gardening, or attending a 12-step meeting. A lot of people attend a 12-step meeting several times a day and in-person in early sobriety. It fills the schedule up, and the activity keeps you mentally and emotionally stimulated.

Shifting focus away from addiction onto something else is key to many recovery models. Paul Earley, founder of the RecoveryMind Training program, emphasizes that addiction behaviors are automatic, ingrained in our neurocircuitry. He explains that recovery involves replacing unhealthy behaviors with more adaptive ones, crowding out the old habits (Earley 2021).

Do something, anything, especially if it takes you out of your current environment. Get active and don't overthink it. While mental health approaches often suggest sitting with your feelings, during intense cravings, action might be a better option. For those with addictions, the times we need activity the most are often when we find excuses not to. This is why structure and staying busy are essential, even when all we want is to stay in bed (Lembke 2021a, 2021b).

However, balance is important; pushing ourselves too hard can lead to burnout and seeking pleasure in unhealthy ways, like overeating. Finding your balance in this arena will be a long-term process.

Play It Forward

In 12-step program recovery circles, people who at risk of relapse are often encouraged by fellows in the program to "play it forward." If you have a craving and find yourself reaching for the cookie, pause and ask yourself, what will happen next? Sure, it might taste good for a second or two, but then you'll want another, and then another. If you end up eating a lot of unhelpful food, how will you feel physically and emotionally afterward?

When we are being truly honest with ourselves, those of us with food addiction quickly realize that feeding the craving will lead us to much darker places than not feeding the craving would.

Exercise: **Playing It Forward**

In a moment of craving, take a time out for ten minutes and do this writing exercise. Ask yourself, if you decide to eat this cookie, what will your life look like in three hours, three days, three months? If you decide not to eat this cookie, what then? Journal or draw out (in images) your answers to these two questions on a piece of paper, using two separate sides of the paper. Describe every facet of your future life as a cookie eater and a non-cookie eater—family, friends, work—in detail. Call a trusted friend and tell them what you came up with, to solidify your thinking even further. You can do a variation on this exercise in moments where you're not craving too, as the more you can remind yourself of the truth, the fewer opportunities your cravings will have to take root.

Urge Surfing

Urge surfing is a mindfulness-based exercise that can help people learn how to be with a craving until it passes. It also helps people gain insight into the fact that cravings are temporary.

However, it's an advanced skill. If you are having a craving and you try urge surfing, and it gets too uncomfortable or you're finding it too hard to resist the craving, return to "get busy" or "play it forward" until you feel strong again.

Exercise: **Urge Surfing**

Find a quiet, safe place and get comfortable. If you want, you can lie down. Center yourself by attending to your breath. After you feel calm, try to find the craving in your body and watch it. Where is it located and how does it feel—is it hot, tingly, jabbing? How does it change as you breathe in and out? Try to visualize your urge like a wave, with the sensations rising at first, then eventually falling off, and then maybe returning for another round. Just notice the wave as it rises and falls, with curiosity and without acting on it. Where does it move in the body over time, and how does it change as the minutes tick by? As you attend to the craving, try to observe it from the perspective of your wise, recovery-oriented mind, which is the part of you that is tuned into the bigger picture of what is best for you in the long run. Tell yourself that this craving is just a craving, but not *my* craving, and this thought to use or consume is just a thought, but not *my* thought. As with any mindfulness exercise, when you become distracted, just note that you are in your thoughts again, and bring your attention back to the feeling of the craving in the body, without judgment. Remind yourself that everything changes, and that with time, the craving will pass.

Visit http://www.newharbinger.com/54681 for handouts containing grounding techniques, and the Resources List for a link to a tool from SMART Recovery called DEADS.

Professional Solutions

If you feel you need more support around food cue sensitivity than what is here, consider seeking specialized help. The bonus chapter "Accessing Professional Help" at http://www.newharbinger.com/54681 has advice on finding a therapist or prescriber, but here are some addiction treatment options that may help reduce cue reactivity.

Cognitive behavioral therapy (CBT)—also known as relapse prevention therapy for addictions—and mindfulness-based relapse prevention therapy are evidence-based methods that help reduce exposure to substance-related cues and manage cue-elicited cravings.

Relapse prevention medications, prescribed by medical providers, may aid in reducing cravings and substance use by dampening the brain's reward response (Wilcox 2021). These medications, which come with moderate risk of side effects, include naltrexone (blocks opioid receptors), topiramate (blocks glutamate AMPA receptors), and GLP-1 receptor agonists like liraglutide and semaglutide. These have been shown to reduce brain reactivity to alcohol cues and lower alcohol use (Klausen et al. 2022; Myrick et al. 2008; Wetherill et al. 2021), and while there are no randomized controlled trials for these medications in relation to food addiction, studies show they can reduce binge eating, promote weight loss, and decrease the brain's reactivity to food cues as well (Konanur et al. 2020; Wang et al. 2014; Wilcox 2021). This suggests they could be useful in preventing relapse in food addiction treatment, particularly regarding food cue sensitivity. For more information about pharmacotherapy pros and cons, access the aforementioned bonus chapter at http://www.newharbinger.com/54681.

CHAPTER 11

Skills to Enhance Emotional Resilience

"Self-compassion increases motivation, overall well-being, and [our] ability to try again...and changes the nervous system...and brain."

—Ann Saffi Biasatti, *Food Junkies Podcast*

You have a food plan and have minimized your exposure to potential triggers in your environment. You're prioritizing sleep and exercise, and while your cravings are better, they're still an issue—especially weeknights after work when you're feeling depleted and irritable. Despite your best efforts, you still turn to comforting, highly rewarding food several nights a week, and you want that to change.

As discussed in Chapters 3–5, addiction is driven by three core brain changes: heightened food-cue sensitivity, difficulty with stress and emotion regulation, and impaired impulse control. This chapter will help you stabilize your emotions so you'll be less tempted to use food for comfort. These skills will also help you cope with withdrawal from highly rewarding foods.

By avoiding trigger foods, you're already making progress: the less you consume, the faster your stress response heals and your emotions stabilize. However, if emotional eating is an issue, you may need additional emotional skills beyond what's required for cue sensitivity alone (Ouwens, van Strien, and van Leeuwe 2009).

In this chapter, you'll learn skills to improve your mood, manage stress, and reduce emotional triggers that lead to cravings. These tools, along with those in chapters 10 and 12, will help you stay on track with your food plan.

Identify Your Triggering Moods

Whether we're in the early stages of withdrawal, recently got a poor night's sleep, or were unjustifiably reprimanded at work, a range of uncomfortable emotions (sadness, anger, irritability, anxiety, depression, fatigue, stress, overwhelm) can activate our desire for highly rewarding food and instigate a landslide. Boredom, shame, and apathy are also common triggers for many of us. Sometimes, even positive mood states (excitement, anticipation, satisfaction, joy) can be triggers, so watch out!

Remember HALTTSS, which stands for Hungry, Angry, Lonely, Tired, Thirsty, Sick, and Stressed. These are states of mind that activate addictive circuits and their corresponding behaviors. I talked about the importance of minimizing your risk of getting hungry, thirsty, and tired in previous chapters; anger, stress, and loneliness also might be triggers of addictive behavior in you, too.

Exercise: Trigger Emotions

List several emotions that often trigger you to seek out highly rewarding food for comfort.

Example: *stressed, overwhelmed, tired, irritable.*

Develop an Emotionally Supportive Community

In chapter 7, we discussed the benefits of joining a recovery community, which can help with addictions by offering hope and inspiration. Community is also key for emotional support, which will also rewire your emotional brain in positive ways and improve mood and stress resilience.

Isolation fuels addictive behaviors. During COVID-19, rates of addiction and weight gain surged globally (Melamed, Selby, and Taylor 2022; Schulte, Kral, and Allison 2022). In the "Rat Park" studies, isolated rats self-administered drugs until they died, while rats in social groups consumed less and survived (Alexander et al. 2024). Community helps mitigate addiction.

Community boosts mood, too. Twelve-step meetings have been shown to reduce depressive symptoms and support sobriety (Wilcox, Pearson, and Tonigan 2015; Wilcox and Tonigan 2018). Group membership "adds more slices to the pie" of what it means to be you (Tabri 2024), fosters a feeling of belonging (Biasetti 2022), and increases confidence and reduces shame if the group is supportive and non-judgmental (Lembke 2021a, 2021b). Are your addictive behaviors triggered by loneliness or boredom? Community of all kinds can help here, too, as it can be a source of simple companionship.

Neuroscience confirms that social connections activate the brain's reward system. Being understood by others releases feel-good chemicals like opioids, oxytocin, and dopamine (Delgado, Fareri, and Chang 2023; Lembke 2021a, 2021b; Lieberman 2022), which reinforce positive behavior (chapter 3). Mirror neurons activate when we observe the emotions of others, helping us connect by creating empathy. This too may be a mechanism by which a recovery-oriented community helps us change our behaviors and beliefs (Ifland 2021; Jaffe 2019).

Communities that can improve emotional resilience include 12-step programs and other spiritual communities. Involving loved ones in your recovery can create a supportive community. Professional support, such as group therapy or counseling, also counts as community (more on this in the professional help chapter at http://www.newharbinger.com/54681). While social groups like hiking or knitting clubs can help, they may lack the emotional openness needed for deep recovery support.

Feel and Name Your Emotions

People with addictions often have difficulty identifying and naming their emotions. Ellen Vora, whose book *The Anatomy of Anxiety* discusses the relationship between anxiety and eating, says about her own recovery, "I had to learn how to cry, like really give myself permission to cry—and that was a much needed release and…it was free therapy (Vora 2022)."

Studies show that teaching people *emotional granularity*—to identify and name their emotions—can reduce addictive behavior (Kashdan et al. 2010). This is a common tool that has been used in recovery circles for decades. Higher emotional granularity has many benefits for a satisfying life, according to emotion researcher and author of *How Emotions are Made* Lisa Feldman Barrett. In a collection of scientific studies, people who could distinguish finely among their unpleasant feelings —those "Fifty shades of feeling crappy"—were more flexible when regulating their emotions, less likely to drink excessively when stressed, and less likely to retaliate aggressively against someone who has hurt them (Barrett 2023; Barrett et al. 2001; Pond et al. 2012; Barrett 2018).

To practice emotional granularity yourself, please visit the online tools at http://www.newharbinger.com/54681 and access the Feelings Wheel. Use it to determine the feeling you are having right now. Remember that a thought is different from a feeling; a thought, like *I am never going to get all this work done by my deadline*, is not the same as the related feeling, which might be "overwhelmed" or "stressed" in this case.

Physical Exercise

Another great way to boost your mood, enhance your stress resilience, and reduce your need to use food for emotional comfort is through physical exercise. In addition to reducing cue reactivity, physical exercise can benefit emotional health by reducing depression, anxiety, and irritability, as well as increasing self-esteem (Wilcox 2021; Robertson et al. 2016; Schuch et al. 2016). One way it does so is by enhancing connectivity between the amygdala, which generates emotions, and the prefrontal cortex, which regulates them (Ge et al. 2021). Recall from chapter 4 that reduced connectivity between these regions is a hallmark of both addictive disorders and depressive and anxiety disorders (Wilcox, Pommy, and Adinoff 2016). When the connectivity is stronger, the prefrontal cortex can dampen the amygdala's response and stabilize your emotional reactions.

Sleep

As is true with physical exercise, getting adequate sleep will also improve your mood and function in your stress reactivity circuits, as well as reduce cue reactivity (Wilcox 2021). Sleep loss negatively affects mood, which increases our drive to comfort eat. Insufficient or erratic sleep is known to exacerbate depression, anxiety, and mood disorders. Getting good sleep keeps you serene and happy.

Personal Development

Another way to enhance your emotional recovery is to cultivate areas of your life outside of food, food addiction, and preoccupation with food. A fulfilling, purpose-driven life, aligned with your life goals and core values, will lessen your sensitivity to stressful stimuli and reduce the temptation to seek solace in highly rewarding food. You'll generally feel better about yourself, and you'll be more rooted in what matters most to you.

Exercise: Considering Your Values

What values matter most to you right now? Values are the qualities that give our lives meaning and guide our actions. Examples of values include creativity, freedom, joy, adventure, connection, health, accomplishment, and peace. Visit http://www.newharbinger.com/54681 for a list of some more common values to get some ideas. Choose ten that resonate with you most.

Next, journal about why each value is important, how your life aligns with it, and where you could improve alignment. Reflect on areas like your career, relationships, hobbies, and self-care. If you're unsure, try journaling on questions like: What's going well in your life? What could be better? Who supports you? How do you spend your leisure time? What role does faith play in your life?

Now narrow down to three values. Once you've identified three, choose one small change you could make this week to live more in line with one of them. For instance, if accomplishment is your value, set a small goal to complete by week's end that would help you feel more accomplished. It can be as simple as "organize the spice rack." Remember that in early recovery, it's best to avoid major changes while your body and mind adjust. Small, manageable changes, like one a week, can have a meaningful impact over time.

Values work can also be a powerful change motivator (Miller and Rollnick 2023). To explore this, journal on how changing a habit would impact your ability to live in alignment with your values. For instance, if your value is "joy" and if you are thinking of cutting out cookies—in the short-term, making this change might reduce your experiences of joy, but, in the long-term, making this change might lead to more joy with fewer cravings and higher energy levels. Let these reflections guide you.

Practice Mindfulness

You've already heard in chapter 10 how mindfulness skills can help you with food cue sensitivity and craving. Mindfulness skills can also help you enhance your emotional resilience and improve your mood. Increasing your awareness of your inner emotional world will build your capacity to accept what is, which will reduce your reflexive habit of using highly rewarding food to feel better.

Studies show mindfulness reduces anxiety and depression symptoms, and mindfulness programs are used as primary treatments for several mental health conditions (Wilcox 2021). Reduction of stress reactivity is believed to be a key mechanism by which mindfulness improves addictive behavior (Kober et al. 2017). Also, like physical exercise, mindfulness increases connectivity between the prefrontal cortex and amygdala, reversing problematic brain wiring in emotional circuits (Wilcox, Pommy, and Adinoff 2016; Goldin et al. 2021; Li et al. 2022).

Exercise: **RAIN**

Next time you experience an intense emotion, try a mindfulness exercise called RAIN. Tara Brach (see her self-compassion exercises in the Resources List at http://www.newharbinger.com/54681) calls this approach "radical acceptance," and describes it as "practicing a conscious effort to acknowledge and honor difficult situations and emotions" (Brach 2003).

Set a timer for ten minutes and sit comfortably with your eyes closed. Focus on your breath, then when you feel ready, begin to explore your inner emotional landscape.

> **R. Recognize:** Identify what you're feeling—anxiety, sadness, guilt? Name the emotions if possible, or simply notice them without judgment.
>
> **A. Allow:** Let the emotions be without trying to fix or change them. Emotions naturally rise and fall; accept them as part of being human.
>
> **I. Investigate:** Notice where the emotion is in your body. Is it in your chest, neck, or stomach? Is it swirly, tight, or stabbing? How does it change with your breath? What does this part of yourself that is experiencing this emotion need right now?
>
> **N. Nurture:** Reassure yourself. Tell yourself it's okay, the feelings will pass, and that you're good. Notice how your body responds to these comforting words.

Lisa Feldman Barrett refers to this process as extreme ownership of our psychological and physical pain and Molly calls it "lean into the suck" (Barrett 2023). By accepting our feelings and focusing in on them rather than distracting ourselves from them, we gain insight and clarity, and sometimes the pain reduces, too.

Be aware that strong emotions in early recovery can also feel overwhelming. If meditation becomes too intense, shift to action, as discussed in chapter 10.

Redraw Your Inner Emotional Landscape

When we lose our quick go-to source of happiness—our highly rewarding food—we often feel sad, despondent, and full of grief, in addition to the psychological symptoms of withdrawal. But as our brain recalibrates, we naturally rediscover the capacity to access joy from other aspects of life.

Exercise: Cultivating Joy

What activities give you joy? Some examples could include friendships and family; nourishing food; pets; reading; watching good movies; wondering at the beauty of little things; music; career and homelife accomplishments; or time in nature. Community, which we've already discussed, is a key source of joy for many of us too.

List out the things in your life that bring you joy. Journal on how you can cultivate that joy daily.

It's Not Your Fault

Thanks to our culture and internalized weight stigma, those of us with food addiction feel responsible for our problem. Self-criticism and excessive perfectionism like this will impair healing from an addiction or eating disorder. Berating ourselves actually blocks new learning and reinforces old neural pathways, bringing us right back to where we started (Biasetti 2022). Critical internal voices stomp on well-being, motivation, and our willingness to try again. They make our moods dark, fuel limbic activity, and increase the chances we will try to use food to feel better.

When you notice yourself spiraling into shame and guilt about your eating issues, remind yourself it's not your willpower that's at fault. Erica LaFata (formerly Schulte) reminds us, "What hasn't changed in the last 50 years is that people haven't lost their willpower skills. [What has changed] is availability of ultra-processed food" (Schulte 2022). A public health crisis got dumped on our innocent, unwitting heads, and those of us with food addiction just have the bad luck of being neurobiologically susceptible. Every time you start blaming yourself, shift your focus from self-blame to the responsibility of the government and the food industry. Keep deemphasizing weight loss and working on your body image, too (chapter 7).

See Slips as Opportunity, Not Failure

When you slip and eat outside your food plan (and you will—whether it's a bite of a cookie, a binge, or months of binges), self-blame is not helpful. You're working to change long-standing patterns, which takes time, commitment, and self-compassion. Even if it takes weeks or years to change your eating habits, you're not alone; you're actually like most people with food addiction. Change is possible, but it takes time—hang in there. It's all part of the process.

Approach slips with curiosity. If you slip often, don't label yourself a "chronic relapser" but a "chronic never-giver-upper." Slips aren't failures; they're chances to learn. What were the triggers? What can you change to better support your recovery? What new tools from this book can you try? Seek support from your recovery community for guidance and input.

Exercise: Making Slips Your Superpower

Here is an abbreviated worksheet for you to use to post-process your slips, thanks to the generosity of Molly, Clarissa, and Sweet Sobriety (https://www.sweetsobriety.ca).

When you have a slip, ask yourself the following questions and journal for several minutes on each of these questions.

1. What was the situation? What happened?
2. What lead up to it? What had I been feeling?
3. What sabotaging thoughts did I have right before I picked up the bite? List as many of these as you can remember.
4. How do I feel now that I have gone back to old behaviors? Be thorough.

The faster you can get back on track with your ideal food plan, the less risk you have of reinforcing your old addictive patterns. Here are some tips:

- Get back on plan at your very next meal.
- Plan, Prepare, Protect: create a structured recovery Plan, Prepare your environment, and Protect your recovery with community support, coping skills, self-care, and accountability.
- Don't allow yourself to get too hungry.
- Strengthen your mindset muscle by solidifying your commitment to this lifestyle for the long term. Recommit to your food plan, incorporating new skills and solutions. Consistent practice will help you replace old, addictive behaviors with healthier ones!

Build Your Self-Compassion Muscle

Remember to treat yourself with compassion. This helps regulate emotions and reduces the power of stress and cravings. Mindfulness practices can support this (chapters 10–11), as well as focusing less on weight loss and more on body image, if relevant (chapter 7). Consider joining a self-compassion community, such as those offered by compassion researcher Kristen Neff (see the Resources List at http://www.newharbinger.com/54681).

Coping Strategies for Strong Emotions

Sometimes, despite our best efforts, strong emotions hit. While emotions are normal and informative, they can trigger cravings or food-seeking behaviors when they become overwhelming. When this happens, try urge surfing or distract yourself with activities (chapter 10) until you feel safe enough to explore your feelings with tools like RAIN or the Feelings Wheel at http://www.newharbinger.com/54681.

Exercise: Overwhelm-Reducing Activities

Here are activities I use when stressed, overwhelmed, or fatigued:

- Drink sparkling water
- Dive into creative work (like writing)
- Take a walk or run
- Call a trusted friend
- Take a nap
- Attend a 12-step meeting
- Do a guided meditation

What activities would you like to try when dealing with overwhelming emotions?

Professional Solutions

Many people with food addiction also deal with depression, anxiety, or trauma-related disorders. If you're finding it hard to stick with your food plan, consider getting evaluated for a psychiatric condition. Counseling or psychotherapy—especially with evidence-based therapies for depression, anxiety, and trauma—might be what you need. Effective therapies include cognitive behavioral therapy (CBT), dynamic psychotherapy, interpersonal psychotherapy, dialectical behavioral therapy (DBT), and mindfulness-based therapy (Wilcox 2021). For trauma, internal family systems therapy (IFS), somatic therapies, and EMDR can be helpful. Mindfulness-based stress reduction courses are widely available and shown to reduce depression and stress. If you're facing relationship challenges, couples or family therapy can help. Even if you're not struggling, couples or family work can help to prepare loved ones for the changes you're making in recovery.

Medication can also stabilize emotions if you're diagnosed with major depressive disorder, generalized anxiety disorder, binge eating disorder, or PTSD. Antidepressants like SSRIs or bupropion, or non-habit-forming antianxiety meds, can relieve emotional distress and reduce food cravings. Fluoxetine in particular may also help with insulin resistance and cause a little weight loss (Serralde-Zuniga et al. 2022).

I didn't think I ate for emotional reasons. I tried paroxetine and escitalopram with little success for mood or eating. However, fluoxetine made my cravings disappear! This taught me that emotions were probably driving my eating to some degree, even when I thought they weren't. If you're struggling, consider an evaluation for a mental health disorder and seek treatment if needed. Consult the bonus chapter on finding professional help at http://www.newharbinger.com/54681.

CHAPTER 12

Skills to Improve Decision Making

"With all addictions…we are brainwashed into believing that our little fix is a source of pleasure or comfort. We are deluded into thinking that happiness lies in the very thing that's causing us misery."

—Allen Carr, *Allen Carr's Easy Way To Quit Emotional Eating* (Carr 2019).

You've got a food plan you're happy with, you've reduced your intake of highly rewarding foods, and you've minimized triggers. You're more resilient to stress, thanks to a daily twenty-minute walk, better sleep, cultivating joy, and viewing slips as learning opportunities. Cravings are lower, but sticking to the plan remains tough. This could be because while you've eased off the "accelerator," your "brakes" still need work, and your mind is full of rationalizations.

As discussed in chapter 5, people with food addiction often struggle with impulse control and have impaired decision making from overconsumption of high sugar ultra-processed food. In this chapter, you'll learn strategies to better regulate impulses and identify self-deceptions that can sabotage your recovery plans.

Techniques to Improve Self-Regulation

Some of the previous techniques we've learned about are useful here as well.

Adequate sleep. Sleep is crucial not only for emotional stability but also for impulse control and decision making. Sleep deprivation weakens concentration, memory, and attention, while enough sleep restores your brain's ability to resist cravings and make better decisions (Samakidou et al. 2023; Wilcox 2021).

Physical activity. Exercise not only reduces sensitivity to food cues and boosts emotional health, but it also improves impulse control and focus. Studies in people with addictions show that exercise restores D2 receptors in the brain and rejuvenates the prefrontal cortex, reducing impulsivity and drug use (Wilcox 2021; Robertson et al. 2016; Wang, Zhou, and Chang 2015).

Community. Community supports recovery by enhancing impulse control and boosting striatal D2 receptor levels, just like exercise (Baez-Mendoza and Schultz 2013; Martinez et al. 2010; Wilcox 2021; Dennis 2021b). Recovery community also helps remind us that food is addictive and mitigates the power of societal messages to lure us back into unhelpful old patterns of thinking and behaving. In most circles, people discount the idea that some food is addictive. Susan Peirce Thompson, in recovery from both stimulants (crack and crystal meth) and food herself, says that food is by far the hardest addiction to quit, partially because of the never-ending cues, but also because the social pressure is much more intense. "You tell people you're quitting drugs, and they pat you on the back. You tell people you're not eating pumpkin pie at Thanksgiving dinner?..." (Thompson 2022). A different story altogether. Surrounding yourself with people who understand food addiction is key to keeping you on track.

Cognitive Reframing

Our minds are filled with unhelpful rationalizations and justifications, which are part of the addictive process (chapter 5). Addressing them is key to rewiring the brain and reducing impulses to eat highly rewarding foods. Cognitive reframing, a core technique of cognitive behavioral therapy (CBT), can help change these distorted thoughts and is an evidence-based approach for treating addiction. Cognitive reframing also boosts prefrontal cortex engagement during cravings and emotional distress, helping you regain self-control (Goldin et al. 2021; Zhao et al. 2012; Yang et al. 2018).

There are two steps in cognitive reframing:

1. **Identify your rationalizations:** Recognize the thoughts that lead to addictive behaviors. The more you understand these misleading thoughts, the better equipped you'll be to resist. As Kathryn Hansen says in *Brain Over Binge*, urges are "neurobiological junk" (Hansen 2016).

2. Remind yourself that these urges and thoughts are lies. Employing mindfulness skills can help you pause and identify these thoughts. Over time, you'll become skilled at letting them pass without acting on them.

3. **Test and reframe:** Challenge these thoughts and rewrite them to align with reality. Reframing helps you reinterpret situations and adjust your thinking.

Exercise: Reframing Unhelpful Thoughts

1. Identify your common rationalizations and false beliefs about highly rewarding food.

Examples of rationalizations:

"My life will be meaningless and joyless without chocolate chip cookies."

"If I don't eat cookies, it means I have an eating disorder because I'm restricting myself."

"You want it, and you shouldn't deprive yourself."

"You'll never stick with it anyway—might as well give in."

"You deserve it; it's a special day—you can start again tomorrow."

"You don't really need to quit—you're being paranoid and compulsive."

"I can have just one cookie; this time will be different because of X."

Spend a week noticing thoughts that lead you to stray from your food plan. Write them down as valuable discoveries.

Sometimes, thoughts may seem like self-care rather than rationalizations. For example, thinking "I just went on a long hike and need more food" might be genuine self-care. Distinguishing between rationalizations and true needs can take time. Be kind to yourself and consider seeking support from an addiction-trained provider or attending a 12-step meeting to work through confusion.

2. Reframe these thoughts.

After identifying your rationalizations, it's time to reframe them.

Pick one rationalization and ask yourself:

- What is the evidence that this thought is false?
- How can I reframe this thought to be more balanced and real?

Example:

"My life will be joyless without chocolate chip cookies."

- **Evidence it's true:** I enjoy the initial moments of eating cookies; there's an intense surge of joy with each bite.
- **Evidence it's false:** After one cookie, I obsess over eating more until I'm uncomfortably full. The joy is fleeting, and afterward, I feel unwell for days, reducing joy from other experiences.
- **Reframed statement:** Eating cookies gives momentary joy, but overall, they subtract joy from my life. There are many other sources of joy, so not having cookies won't remove joy from my life. This is just withdrawal talking; soon, I'll find healthier ways to experience joy if I stay committed. (Greenberger and Padesky 2015)

Writing these down in advance helps when you're triggered. Note them as they arise, especially if you've gone off course. Celebrate when you catch them. Read them often to become savvy about your justifications. Instead of criticizing yourself for having them, learn to work with them. The more you recognize their forms, the less susceptible you'll be in the moment.

Avoid Addictive Substances

We haven't discussed this much, but it's a crucial topic: avoid using other addictive substances like alcohol, cigarettes, or marijuana as replacements for highly rewarding foods. These substances impact brain wiring and compromise impulse control and decision making, just like highly rewarding food does.

In early food addiction recovery, abstaining from these substances can feel especially hard. People often switch to another addiction—this is called addiction transfer or cross addiction (Wilcox 2021). Be mindful of this. Having an extra glass of wine to cope may seem harmless, but it increases impulsivity and can make you more vulnerable to triggers, potentially undermining your food recovery goals. Don't hesitate to get help from a professional for comorbid addictions (see the bonus chapter on this topic at http://www.newharbinger.com/54681).

Professional Solutions

Therapy can be very helpful if you struggle with impulse control and rationalizations. Professional help can improve cognitive reframing skills, aiding in better decision making. CBT, relapse prevention, and mindfulness-based relapse prevention are effective, evidence-based options (Greenberger and Padesky 2015; Bowen et al. 2021; Wilcox 2021).

Sometimes, it's unclear whether our decisions are aligned with our best interests or sneakily influenced by addiction. As Susan Peirce Thompson astutely mused on *Food Junkies*, "How do you know you're not being tricked? I have a brain that doesn't always have my best interests at heart" (Thompson 2022).

Internal family systems (IFS) therapy is a type of psychotherapy rooted in the idea that our psyche is comprised of parts, which can disagree about the best course of action to take in our lives. Our parts are individual to each of us, discoverable through therapy, mindfulness, and self-reflection (Thompson 2022). I recommend you check out a book about self-guided IFS, if this approach interests you (Earley 2022).

According to IFS, most of us with food addiction have an addicted part (which lunges for food in a pinch) and a restrictor/dieter part (which responds to a binge by counting calories and berating ourselves). Neither of these parts operating in isolation necessarily help us in the long run. But each has our best interest in mind. The best place to be is somewhere in the middle, where the more helpful needs and drives of both opposing parts can be met.

The part of ourselves that has an overview of all the needs of our various parts and can integrate them is called the "Self." According to IFS, you know you're operating from the Self when you're manifesting the 8 C's: Compassion, Creativity, Curiosity, Confidence, Courage, Calm, Connectedness, and Clarity (Thompson 2022). Making decisions from that place means your program is probably on track. Consulting a therapist that does this kind of work might be of value to you, if this concept resonates.

If you have a diagnosis like ADHD (common in addiction and binge eating), medication may also improve attention and impulse control. Medications like bupropion, lisdexamfetamine, and GLP-1 agonists act on impulse control and cognitive function in conditions like binge eating, addiction, and obesity, studies show (Wilcox 2021; McIntyre et al. 2013; Holscher 2024). For more information on seeking professional help, visit the bonus chapter at http://www.newharbinger.com/54681.

In chapters 10–12, you've learned many tools. Start with one or two and see what works for you. You have plenty of options, so don't give up—good luck!

Conclusion

Although research has established the addictiveness of certain foods and many people experience recovery from overeating through addiction-based treatment models, food addiction has not yet been made an official diagnosis. Consequently, limited research exists on how best to treat it. This is a terrible shame, given that food addiction is more problematic than obesity (Minhas et al. 2021), and its presence makes eating disorders much harder to treat (LaFata and Gearhardt 2022). Evidence-based solutions are needed, and *now*.

This book tells you what we know today about how you can get well. Although much of what I offer in this book treatment-wise is not yet backed by large-scale, randomized, controlled clinical trials, its concepts are firmly rooted in solid research from the substance use and eating disorders fields. I've attempted to amass the most updated and best information we have.

But you should know that the field is changing fast. The food addiction concept has gained a significant amount of traction in the last decade, and it continues to grow roots. George Koob, director of the NIAAA, and Nora Volkow, director of the National Institute on Drug Abuse (NIDA), presented a continuing medical education course for the American Psychiatric Association this year entitled "Food Addiction: A New Substance Use Disorder" (Koob et al. 2024). Organized efforts are underway to find consensus (Unwin et al. 2024; Gearhardt 2024) among prominent food addiction providers, scientists, nutritionists, and eating disorder treatment providers around issues such as what to call it ("ultra-processed food use disorder" is popular), whether to include it in the DSM and the International Classification of Diseases (ICD), and needs for research; to this end the International Food Addiction Consensus Conference held its first meeting highly successful meeting in May of 2024 and the recording is available online (https://the-chc.org/fas/conference). Hopefully, efforts to change policy and curb the misinformation spread by Big Food and Big Pharma will persist and someday win out.

I hope that food addiction will be officialized soon. Once that happens, research funding will start flowing into the field, more treatment studies will be done, and public health efforts to curb availability of ultra-processed food will be taken more seriously by government agencies. I can't wait to see how future research and mainstream acceptance of food addiction will impact public health in the coming decades.

And now, back to you, for whom I wrote this book. I hope it's provided some valuable insights, and that you've found some practical tools that resonate for you.

Let's return, for a moment, to your recovery goals in chapter 7. How would you rate your progress on these goals? What needs to be tweaked? This recovery thing is an ongoing process; it may take years to fine-tune your approach. That's totally normal. Like they say in AA, "Keep coming back."

Remember, too, that there is more great material online—don't skip the online tools at http://www.newharbinger.com/54681! There you'll find a resource list, two bonus chapters on supplemental treatment, which most of us end up needing at some point or another, and additional tools to use to help you manage your cravings and rewire your brain back to health to get free.

Be well as you embark on this journey. Be kind to yourself. And perhaps above all, have fun!

Acknowledgments

First, I want to acknowledge the three *amazing* women who have spearheaded the *Food Junkies Podcast*: Vera Tarman, Clarissa Kennedy, and Molly Painschab. What they have done and continue to do is of great importance, transforming the face of healthcare from the bottom up through their interviews of specialists and experts from around the world. The result is a masterpiece; their tireless dedication gives thousands of people with food addiction a way out.

When I first started listening to the *Food Junkies Podcast* in October 2022, it blew my mind. I believed in food addiction—in fact, I'd written a textbook on it—but I didn't have a professional or even personal community to share ideas with. Though I had found a significant amount of relief for myself by letting go of sugar, I was still questioning the concept because I was struggling with some foods and had doubts that I'd ever get completely free.

But the podcast helped me internalize emotionally what I already knew cognitively: that I wasn't alone, that I wasn't "crazy," and that my brain was just biologically different in the way it responded to certain foods. It helped me let go of maple syrup and all-fruit jelly, which were causing me all sorts of trouble.

The podcast has also enriched my professional world, teaching me things about neuroscience, nutrition science, public policy, treatment centers, experienced practitioners, and novel interventions I'd never known or heard about.

I want to extend specific thanks to Clarissa for all of her help in writing the book. She has worked alongside me tirelessly as I put the book together. She's played both editor and sounding board, providing crucial materials for the food plan and key content through worksheets, quotes, and ideas. Her wealth of wisdom from her clinical experience and her work on the podcast have been invaluable, as well as her magnificent way with words. I couldn't have done it without her.

Thank you to both Clarissa and Molly for sharing handouts and food plan materials from Sweet Sobriety to repurpose for this book. And thank you to Vera for her courage in writing the book *Food Junkies* during a time when the medical community was less open to the concept of food addiction; her book is a must-read and a cornerstone of the field.

Also, my enthusiastic thanks to the team at New Harbinger. Vicraj Gill, I can't express my gratitude enough for your extensive, invaluable feedback and help in making a complex topic more digestible. Thanks as well to Jed Bickman, Marisa Solis, and Rebecca Job.

I also want to acknowledge all the professionals—mostly guests on *Food Junkies*—who have devoted their careers to food addiction through writing, research, and clinical and public health efforts; you are helping to change the world for the better. Thanks to Nicole Avena, Erica LaFata, Ashley Gearhardt, Nora Volkow, and George Koob for the neuroscience establishing that food is addictive. Thanks to Michael Moss, Chris van Tulleken, Gary Taubes, and Robert Lustig for continuing to hold the food industry accountable and spearhead public health efforts to curb ultra-processed food. Thanks to Amy Reichelt for her help with the food plan. Thanks to David Wiss, Kim Dennis, and Timothy Brewerton for their ongoing efforts to bridge the food addiction and eating disorders treatment camps.

Finally, thank you to Bill, my partner, and numerous other family and friends for giving me support and being patient with my absences as I completed this project.

References

Alcoholics Anonymous. 2001. *The Big Book of Alcoholics Anonymous*. 4th ed. New York: Alcoholics Anonymous World Services.

Alexander, B. K., B. L. Beyerstein, P. F. Hadaway, and R. B. Coambs. 1981. "Effect of Early and Later Colony Housing on Oral Ingestion of Morphine in Rats." *Pharmacology, Biochemisty, and Behavior* 15 (4): 571–576.

American Psychiatric Association. 2013. *Diagnostic and Statistical Manual of Mental Disorders, Fifth Edition: DSM-5*. 5th ed. Washington, DC: American Psychiatric Association.

American Psychiatric Association. 2024. "Alcohol Use Disorder." Accessed January 3, 2024. https://www.psychiatry.org/patients-families/alcohol-use-disorder.

Avena, N. 2021. "Episode 15: Dr. Nicole Avena," in *Food Junkies Podcast*, April 9, 2021. 0:55, https://www.foodjunkiespodcast.com/episodes/episode-15-dr-nicole-avena.

Baez-Mendoza, R., and W. Schultz. 2013. "The role of the striatum in social behavior." *Frontiers in Neuroscience* 7: 233.

Bayes, J., J. Schloss, and D. Sibbritt. 2022. "The Effect of a Mediterranean Diet on the Symptoms of Depression in Young Males (the "AMMEND: A Mediterranean Diet in MEN with Depression" study): a Randomized Controlled Trial." *American Journal of Clinical Nutrition* 116 (2): 572–580.

Becetti, I., E. L. Bwenyi, I. E. de Araujo, J. Ard, J. F. Cryan, I. S. Farooqi et. al. 2023. "The Neurobiology of Eating Behavior in Obesity: Mechanisms and Therapeutic Targets: A Report from the 23rd Annual Harvard Nutrition Obesity Symposium." *American Journal of Clinical Nutrition* 118 (1): 314–328.

Bechara, A. 2005. "Decision making, impulse control and loss of willpower to resist drugs: a neurocognitive perspective." *Nature Neuroscience* 8: 1458-63.

Beecher, K., I. Alvarez Cooper, J. Wang, S. B. Walters, F. Chehrehasa, S. E. Bartlett, and A. Belmer. 2021. "Long-Term Overconsumption of Sugar Starting at Adolescence Produces Persistent Hyperactivity and Neurocognitive Deficits in Adulthood." *Frontiers in Neuroscience* 15: 670430.

Biasetti, A. S. 2022. "Episode 77: Dr. Ann Saffi Biasetti," in *Food Junkies Podcast*, June 30, 2022. 1:01, https://www.foodjunkiespodcast.com/episodes/episode-77-dr-ann-saffi-biasetti.

Bikman, B. 2022. "Episode 91: Dr. Ben Bikman," in *Food Junkies Podcast*, September 21, 2022. 1:01, https://www.foodjunkiespodcast.com/episodes/episode-91-dr-ben-bikman.

Blackwell, K. T., A. G. Salinas, P. Tewatia, B. English, J. Hellgren Kotaleski, and D. M. Lovinger. 2019. "Molecular Mechanisms Underlying Striatal Synaptic Plasticity: Relevance to Chronic Alcohol Consumption and Seeking." *European Journal of Neuroscience* 49 (6): 768–783.

Bouton, M. E., S. Maren, and G. P. McNally. 2021. "Behavioral and Neurobiological Mechanisms of Pavlovian and Instrumental Extinction Learning." *Physiological Reviews* 101 (2): 611–681.

Bowen, S., N. Chawla, J. Grow, and G. A. Marlatt. 2021. *Mindfulness-Based Relapse Prevention for Addictive Behaviors: A Clinician's Guide.* 2nd ed. New York: Guilford Press.

Bowen, S., K. Witkiewitz, S. L. Clifasefi, J. Grow, N. Chawla, S. H. Hsu et al. 2014. "Relative Efficacy of Mindfulness-Based Relapse Prevention, Standard Relapse Prevention, and Treatment as Usual for Substance Use Disorders: A Randomized Clinical Trial." *JAMA Psychiatry* 71 (5): 547–556.

Brach, T. 2003. *Radical Acceptance: Awakening the Love That Heals Fear and Shame.* New York: Random House.

Brewerton, T. 2022. "Episode 63: Dr. Timothy Brewerton," in *Food Junkies Podcast*, March 8, 2022. 0:52, https://www.foodjunkiespodcast.com/episodes/episode-63-dr-timothy-brewerton.

Brown, R. 2022. "Episode 103: Dr. Rachel Brown," in *Food Junkies Podcast*, December 14, 2022. 0:56, https://www.foodjunkiespodcast.com/episodes/episode-103-dr-rachel-brown.

Callahan, A. 2023. "What Can We Do About Ultraprocessed Foods?" Knowable, September 20, 2023. https://knowablemagazine.org/content/article/food-environment/2023/what-can-we-do-about-ultraprocessed-foods.

Carmel, M. 2021. "Episode 16: Molly Carmel," in *Food Junkies Podcast*, April 15, 2021. 0:58, https://www.foodjunkiespodcast.com/episodes/episode-160-molly-carmel.

Carr, A. 2019. *Allen Carr's Easy Way to Quit Emotional Eating.* London: Arcturus.

Cortese, S., and L. Tessari. 2017. "Attention-Deficit/Hyperactivity Disorder (ADHD) and Obesity: Update 2016." *Current Psychiatry Reports* 19 (1): 4.

Cranford, J. 2021. "Episode 08: Johnathan Cranford," in *Food Junkies Podcast*, February 18, 2021. 0:49, https://www.foodjunkiespodcast.com/episodes/episode-08-johnathan-cranford.

Davis, C. 2023. "Episode 145: Dr. Caroline Davis," in *Food Junkies Podcast*, October 5, 2023. 0:46, https://www.foodjunkiespodcast.com/episodes/episode-145-caroline-davis.

de Araujo, I. E., J. G. Ferreira, L. A. Tellez, X. Ren, and C. W. Yeckel. 2012. "The Gut-Brain Dopamine Axis: A Regulatory System for Caloric Intake." *Physiology & Behavior* 106 (3): 394–399.

Delgado, M. R., D. S. Fareri, and L. J. Chang. 2023. "Characterizing the Mechanisms of Social Connection." *Neuron* 111 (24): 3911–3925.

Dennis, K. 2021a. "Episode 51: Dr. Kim Dennis (Part 1)," in *Food Junkies Podcast*, December 13, 2021. 0:48, https://www.foodjunkiespodcast.com/episodes/episode-51-dr-kim-dennis-part-1.

Dennis, K. 2021b. "Episode 52: Dr. Kim Dennis (Part 2)," in *Food Junkies Podcast*, December 21, 2021. 0:54, https://www.foodjunkiespodcast.com/episodes/episode-52-dr-kim-dennis-part-2.

Dera, A. M., T. Shen, A. E. Thackray, E. C. Hinton, J. A. King, L. James et al. 2023. "The Influence of Physical Activity on Neural Responses to Visual Food Cues in Humans: A Systematic Review of Functional Magnetic Resonance Imaging Studies." *Neuroscience and Biobehavioral Reviews* 152: 105247.

References

DesMaisons, K. 2022. "Episode 59: Kathleen DesMaisons, PhD," in *Food Junkies Podcast*, February 10, 2022. 1:11, https://www.foodjunkiespodcast.com/episodes/episode-59-kathleen-desmaisons-phd.

di Giacomo, E., F. Aliberti, F. Pescatore, M. Santorelli, R. Pessina, V. Placenti, F. Colmegna, and M. Clerici. 2022. "Disentangling Binge Eating Disorder and Food Addiction: A Systematic Review and Meta-Analysis." *Eating and Weight Disorders* 27 (6): 1963–1970.

Earley, Jay. 2022. *Self-Therapy: A Step-by-Step Guide to Creating Wholeness Using IFS, A Cutting-Edge Psychotherapy*. 3rd ed. Larkspur, CA: Pattern System Books.

Earley, Paul. 2021. "Episode 29: Dr. Paul Earley," in *Food Junkies Podcast*, July 15, 2021. 1:00, https://www.foodjunkiespodcast.com/episodes/episode-29-dr-paul-earley.

Fazzino, T. L., K. Rohde, and D. K. Sullivan. 2019. "Hyper-Palatable Foods: Development of a Quantitative Definition and Application to the US Food System Database." *Obesity* 27 (11): 1761–1768.

Feldman Barrett, L. 2023. "Episode 153: Dr. Lisa Feldman Barrett," in *Food Junkies Podcast*, November 29, 2023. 1:00, https://www.foodjunkiespodcast.com/episodes/episode-153-dr-lisa-feldman-barrett.

———. 2018. "Try These Two Smart Techniques to Help You Master Your Emotions." ideas.ted.com, June 21, 2018. https://ideas.ted.com/try-these-two-smart-techniques-to-help-you-master-your-emotions/.

Feldman Barrett, L. J. Gross, T. C. Christensen, and M. Benvenuto. 2001. "Knowing What You're Feeling and Knowing What to Do About It: Mapping the Relation Between Emotion Differentiation and Emotion Regulation." *Cognition and Emotion* 15 (6): 713–724.

Flint, A. J., A. N. Gearhardt, W. R. Corbin, K. D. Brownell, A. E. Field, and E. B. Rimm. 2014. "Food-Addiction Scale Measurement in 2 Cohorts of Middle-Aged and Older Women." *American Journal of Clinical Nutrition* 99 (3): 578–586.

Freshwell Low Carb Project. 2023. "Dr Unwin's Sugar Infographics." Last updated July 18, 2023. https://lowcarbfreshwell.com/what-is-a-low-carb-lifestyle/dr-unwins-sugar-infographics/.

Garvey, W. T. 2022. "Is Obesity or Adiposity-Based Chronic Disease Curable: The Set Point Theory, the Environment, and Second-Generation Medications." *Endocrine Practice* 28 (2): 214–222.

Ge, L. K., Z. Hu, W. Wang, P. M. Siu, and G. X. Wei. 2021. "Aerobic Exercise Decreases Negative Affect by Modulating Orbitofrontal-Amygdala Connectivity in Adolescents." *Life* 11 (6).

Gearhardt, A. N. 2024. "Episode 191: Dr. Ashley Gearhardt, Ph.D.," in *Food Junkies Podcast*, August 21, 2024. 0:57, https://www.foodjunkiespodcast.com/episodes/episode-191-dr-ashley-gearhardt-phd.

Gearhardt, A. N., W. R. Corbin, and K. D. Brownell. 2016. "Development of the Yale Food Addiction Scale Version 2.0." *Psychology of Addictive Behaviors* 30 (1): 113–121.

Gearhardt, A. N., and E. M. Schulte. 2021. "Is Food Addictive? A Review of the Science." *Annual Review of Nutrition* 41: 387–410.

Gearhardt, A. N., G. J. Wang, G. F. Koob, and N. Volkow. 2024. "Food Addiction: A New Substance Use Disorder." Continuing Medical Education course, American Psychiatric Association.

Gideon, N., N. Hawkes, J. Mond, R. Saunders, K. Tchanturia, and L. Serpell. 2016. "Development and Psychometric Validation of the EDE-QS, a 12 Item Short Form of the Eating Disorder Examination Questionnaire (EDE-Q)." *PLoS One* 11 (5): e0152744.

Goldin, P. R., M. Thurston, S. Allende, C. Moodie, M. L. Dixon, R. G. Heimberg, and J. J. Gross. 2021. "Evaluation of Cognitive Behavioral Therapy vs Mindfulness Meditation in Brain Changes During Reappraisal and Acceptance Among Patients With Social Anxiety Disorder: A Randomized Clinical Trial." *JAMA Psychiatry* 78 (10): 1134–1142.

Gomes Gonçalves, N., N. Vidal Ferreira, N. Khandpur, E. Martinez Steele, R. Bertazzi Levy, P. Andrade Lotufo, et al. 2023. "Association Between Consumption of Ultraprocessed Foods and Cognitive Decline." *JAMA Neurology* 80 (2): 142–150.

Goran, M., and N. M. Avena. 2021. "Episode 38: Dr. Michael Goran and Dr. Nicole Avena (Encore)," in *Food Junkies Podcast*, September 14, 2021. 0:56, https://www.foodjunkiespodcast.com/episodes/episode-38-dr-michael-goran-and-dr-nicole-avena-encore.

Gray, S. M., R. I. Meijer, and E. J. Barrett. 2014. "Insulin Regulates Brain Function, but How Does It Get There?" *Diabetes* 63 (12): 3992–3997.

Greenberger, D., and C. Padesky. 2015. *Mind Over Mood: Change How You Feel by Changing the Way You Think*. New York: Guilford Press.

Greenblatt, J. M. 2022. "Episode 99: Dr. James M. Greenblatt," in *Food Junkies Podcast*, November 18, 2022. 0:47, https://www.foodjunkiespodcast.com/episodes/episode-99-dr-james-m-greenblatt.

Guyenet, S. 2022a. "Episode 78: Dr. Stephan Guyenet (Part 1)," in *Food Junkies Podcast*, June 22, 2022. 0:53, https://www.foodjunkiespodcast.com/episodes/episode-78-dr-stephan-guyenet.

———. 2022b. "Episode 79: Dr. Stephan Guyenet (Part 2)," in *Food Junkies Podcast*, June 28, 2022. 0:59, https://www.foodjunkiespodcast.com/episodes/episode-79-dr-stephan-guyenet-part-2.

Hales, C. M., M. D. Carroll, C. D. Fryar, and C. L. Ogden. 2020. *Prevalence of Obesity and Severe Obesity Among Adults: United States, 2017–2018*. NCHS Data Brief no. 360. Hyattsville, MD: National Center for Health Statistics.

Hall, K. D., A. Ayuketah, R. Brychta, H. Cai, T. Cassimatis, K. Y. Chen et al. 2019. "Ultra-Processed Diets Cause Excess Calorie Intake and Weight Gain: An Inpatient Randomized Controlled Trial of Ad Libitum Food Intake." *Cell Metabolism* 30 (1): 67–77 e3.

Hansen, K. 2016. The *Brain over Binge Recovery Guide: A Simple and Personalized Plan for Ending Bulimia and Binge Eating Disorder*. New Smyrna Beach, FL: Camellia Publishing.

Hauck, C., A. Weiss, E. M. Schulte, A. Meule, and T. Ellrott. 2017. "Prevalence of 'Food Addiction' as Measured with the Yale Food Addiction Scale 2.0 in a Representative German Sample and Its Association with Sex, Age and Weight Categories." *Obesity Facts* 10 (1): 12–24.

Hebb, D. O. 1949. *The Organization of Behavior: A Neuropsychological Theory*. New York: Wiley and Sons.

Hölscher, C. 2024. "Glucagon-Like Peptide-1 Class Drugs Show Clear Protective Effects in Parkinson's and Alzheimer's Disease Clinical Trials: A Revolution in the Making?" *Neuropharmacology* 253: 109952.

References

Hoover, L. V., H. P. Yu, J. R. Cummings, S. G. Ferguson, and A. N. Gearhardt. 2023. "Co-Occurrence of Food Addiction, Obesity, Problematic Substance Use, and Parental History of Problematic Alcohol Use." *Psychology of Addictive Behaviors* 37 (7): 928–935.

Hoover, L. V., H. P. Yu, E. R. Duval, and A. N. Gearhardt. 2022. "Childhood Trauma and Food Addiction: The Role of Emotion Regulation Difficulties and Gender Differences." *Appetite* 177: 106137.

Iceta, S., C. Rodrigue, M. Legendre, J. Daoust, V. Flaudias, A. Michaud, and C. Begin. 2021. "Cognitive Function in Binge Eating Disorder and Food Addiction: A Systematic Review and Three-Level Meta-Analysis." *Progress in Neuropsychopharmacology and Biolgical Psychiatry* 111: 110400.

Ifland, J. R., H. G. Preuss, M. T. Marcus, K. M. Rourke, W. C. Taylor, K. Burau, W. S. Jacobs, W. Kadish, and G. Manso. 2009. "Refined Food Addiction: A Classic Substance Use Disorder." *Medical Hypotheses* 72 (5): 518–526.

Ifland, J. 2021. "Episode 26: Dr. Joan Ifland," in *Food Junkies Podcast*, June 22, 2021. 1:02, https://www.foodjunkiespodcast.com/episodes/episode-26-dr-joan-ifland.

Jaffe, A. 2019. "A Look in the Mirror Neuron: Empathy and Addiction." Psychology Today, July 17, 2019. https://www.psychologytoday.com/us/blog/all-about-addiction/201907/a-look-in-the-mirror-neuron-empathy-and-addiction.

Janes, A. C., M. Datko, A. Roy, B. Barton, S. Druker, C. Neal, K. Ohashi, H. Benoit, R. van Lutterveld, and J. A. Brewer. 2019. "Quitting starts in the brain: a randomized controlled trial of app-based mindfulness shows decreases in neural responses to smoking cues that predict reductions in smoking." *Neuropsychopharmacology* 44 (9): 1631–1638.

Johnstone, J. M., I. Hatsu, G. Tost, P. Srikanth, L. P. Eiterman, A. M. Bruton, et al. 2022. "Micronutrients for Attention-Deficit/Hyperactivity Disorder in Youths: A Placebo-Controlled Randomized Clinical Trial." *Journal of the American Academy of Child and Adolescent Psychiatry* 61 (5): 647–661.

Kahneman, D. 2011. *Thinking, Fast and Slow.* New York: Farrar, Straus and Giroux.

Kaplan, B. J., J. J. Rucklidge, A. R. Romijn, and M. Dolph. 2015. "A Randomised Trial of Nutrient Supplements to Minimise Psychological Stress After a Natural Disaster." *Psychiatry Research* 228 (3): 373–379.

Kaplan, B. J. 2023. "Episode 147: Bonnie J. Kaplan, PhD," in *Food Junkies Podcast*, October 20, 2023. 1:03, https://www.foodjunkiespodcast.com/episodes/episode-147-bonnie-kaplan.

Kashdan, T. B., P. Ferssizidis, R. L. Collins, and M. Muraven. 2010. "Emotion Differentiation as Resilience Against Excessive Alcohol Use: An Ecological Momentary Assessment in Underage Social Drinkers." *Psycholgical Science* 21 (9): 1341–1347.

Katsunuma, R., K. Oba, S. Kitamura, Y. Motomura, Y. Terasawa, K. Nakazaki, A. Hida, Y. Moriguchi, and K. Mishima. 2017. "Unrecognized Sleep Loss Accumulated in Daily Life Can Promote Brain Hyperreactivity to Food Cue." *Sleep* 40 (10).

Katz, D.L. 2023. "Episode 152: Dr. David Katz," in *Food Junkies Podcast*, November 23, 2023. 1:15, https://www.foodjunkiespodcast.com/episodes/episode-152-dr-david-katz.

Kelly, J.F. 2024. "Episode 173: Dr. John Kelly, Ph.D., ABPP," in *Food Junkies Podcast*, April 18, 2024. 0:50, https://www.foodjunkiespodcast.com/episodes/episode-173-dr-john-kelly.

Kemp, J. V. A., V. Kumar, A. Saleem, G. Hashman, M. Hussain, and V. H. Taylor. 2023. "Examining Associations Between Women's Mental Health and Obesity." *Psychiatric Clinics of North America* 46 (3): 539–549.

Klausen, M. K., M. E. Jensen, M. Møller, N. Le Dous, A. Østergaard Jensen, V. A. Zeeman et al. 2022. "Exenatide Once Weekly for Alcohol Use Disorder Investigated in a Randomized, Placebo-Controlled Clinical Trial." *JCI Insight* 7 (19): e159863.

Kober, H., J. A. Brewer, K. L. Height, and R. Sinha. 2017. "Neural Stress Reactivity Relates to Smoking Outcomes and Differentiates Between Mindfulness and Cognitive-Behavioral Treatments." *Neuroimage* 151: 4–13.

Konanur, V. R., T. M. Hsu, S. E. Kanoski, M. R. Hayes, and M. F. Roitman. 2020. "Phasic Dopamine Responses to a Food-Predictive Cue Are Suppressed by the Glucagon-Like Peptide-1 Receptor Agonist Exendin-4." *Physiology and Behavior* 215: 112771.

Koob, G. F. 2022. "Anhedonia, Hyperkatifeia, and Negative Reinforcement in Substance Use Disorders." *Current Topics in Behavioral Neurosciences* 58: 147–165.

Koob, G. F., A. N. Gearhardt, G. J. Wang, and N. Volkow. 2024. "Food Addiction: A New Substance Use Disorder." Continuing Medical Education course, American Psychiatric Association.

Kubzansky, L. D., P. Bordelois, H. J. Jun, A. L. Roberts, M. Cerda, N. Bluestone, and K. C. Koenen. 2014. "The Weight of Traumatic Stress: A Prospective Study of Posttraumatic Stress Disorder Symptoms and Weight Status in Women." *JAMA Psychiatry* 71 (1): 44–51.

LaFata, E. M., and A. N. Gearhardt. 2022. "Ultra-Processed Food Addiction: An Epidemic?" *Psychotherapy and Psychosomatics* 91 (6): 363–372.

Lembke, A. 2021a. *Dopamine Nation: Finding Balance in the Age of Indulgence*. New York: Dutton.

———. 2021b. "Episode 41: Dr. Anna Lembke," in *Food Junkies Podcast*, October 7, 2021. 1:02, https://www.foodjunkiespodcast.com/episodes/episode-41-dr-anna-lembke.

Lewis-Marlow, R. 2023. "Episode 126: Rachel Lewis-Marlow," in *Food Junkies Podcast*, May 24, 2023. 1:00, https://www.foodjunkiespodcast.com/episodes/episode-126-rachel-lewis-marlow.

Li, H., W. Yan, Q. Wang, L. Liu, X. Lin, X. Zhu et al. 2022. "Mindfulness-Based Cognitive Therapy Regulates Brain Connectivity in Patients With Late-Life Depression." *Frontiers in Psychiatry* 13: 841461.

Lieberman, Daniel. 2022. "Episode 98: Dr. Daniel Lieberman," in *Food Junkies Podcast*, November 10, 2022. 0:57, https://www.foodjunkiespodcast.com/episodes/episode-98-dr-daniel-lieberman.

Loper, H., M. Leinen, L. Bassoff, J. Sample, M. Romero-Ortega, K. J. Gustafson, D. M. Taylor, and M. A. Schiefer. 2021. "Both High Fat and High Carbohydrate Diets Impair Vagus Nerve Signaling of Satiety." *Scientific Reports* 11: 10394.

Löwel, S., and W. Singer. 1992. "Selection Of Intrinsic Horizontal Connections In The Visual Cortex By Correlated Neuronal Activity." *Science* 255 (5041): 209–212.

Lustig, Robert. 2021. "Episode 22: Dr. Robert Lustig," in *Food Junkies Podcast*, May 27, 2021. 0:55, https://www.foodjunkiespodcast.com/episodes/episode-22-dr-robert-lustig.

Markus, C. R., G. Panhuysen, A. Tuiten, H. Koppeschaar, D. Fekkes, and M. L. Peters. 1998. "Does Carbohydrate-Rich, Protein-Poor Food Prevent a Deterioration of Mood and Cognitive Performance of Stress-Prone Subjects When Subjected to a Stressful Task?" *Appetite* 31 (1): 49–65.

References

Martinez, D., D. Orlowska, R. Narendran, M. Slifstein, F. Liu, D. Kumar, A. Broft, R. Van Heertum, and H. D. Kleber. 2010. "Dopamine Type 2/3 Receptor Availability in the Striatum and Social Status in Human Volunteers." *Biological Psychiatry* 67 (3): 275–278.

McIntyre, R. S., A. M. Powell, O. Kaidanovich-Beilin, J. K. Soczynska, M. Alsuwaidan, H. O. Woldeyohannes, A. S. Kim, and L. A. Gallaugher. 2013. "The Neuroprotective Effects of GLP-1: Possible Treatments for Cognitive Deficits in Individuals with Mood Disorders." *Behavioural Brain Research* 237: 164–171.

Mehr, J. B., D. Mitchison, H. E. Bowrey, and M. H. James. 2021. "Sleep Dysregulation in Binge Eating Disorder and 'Food Addiction': The Orexin (Hypocretin) System as a Potential Neurobiological Link." *Neuropsychopharmacology* 46: 2051-2061.

Melamed, O. C., P. Selby, and V. H. Taylor. 2022. "Mental Health and Obesity During the COVID-19 Pandemic." *Current Obesity Reports* 11 (1): 23–31.

Meseri, R., and C. Akanalci. 2020. "Food Addiction: A Key Factor Contributing to Obesity?" *Journal of Research in Medical Sciences* 25: 71.

Miller, W. R., and S. Rollnick. 2023. *Motivational Interviewing: Helping People Change and Grow*. 4th ed. New York: Guilford Press.

Minhas, M., C. M. Murphy, I. M. Balodis, A. V. Samokhvalov, and J. MacKillop. 2021. "Food Addiction in a Large Community Sample of Canadian Adults: Prevalence and Relationship with Obesity, Body Composition, Quality of Life and Impulsivity." *Addiction* 116 (10): 2870–2879.

Moberg, K. U. 2022. "Episode 97: Dr. Kerstin Uvnäs Moberg," in *Food Junkies Podcast*, November 2, 2022. 1:07, https://www.foodjunkiespodcast.com/episodes/episode-97-dr-kerstin-uvns-moberg.

Monteiro, C. A., G. Cannon, R. B. Levy, J. C. Moubarac, M. L. Louzada, F. Rauber et al. 2019. "Ultra-Processed Foods: What They Are and How to Identify Them." *Public Health Nutrition* 22 (5): 936–941.

Morales, I., and K. C. Berridge. 2020. "'Liking' and 'Wanting' in Eating and Food Reward: Brain Mechanisms and Clinical Implications." *Physiology and Behavior* 227: 113152.

Moss, Michael. 2021. "Episode 13: Michael Moss," in *Food Junkies Podcast*, March 25, 2021. 1:04, https://www.foodjunkiespodcast.com/episodes/episode-13-michael-moss.

Motomura, Y., R. Katsunuma, M. Yoshimura, and K. Mishima. 2017. "Two Days' Sleep Debt Causes Mood Decline During Resting State Via Diminished Amygdala-Prefrontal Connectivity." *Sleep* 40 (10).

Motomura, Y., S. Kitamura, K. Nakazaki, K. Oba, R. Katsunuma, Y. Terasawa, A. Hida, Y. Moriguchi, and K. Mishima. 2017. "Recovery from Unrecognized Sleep Loss Accumulated in Daily Life Improved Mood Regulation via Prefrontal Suppression of Amygdala Activity." *Frontiers in Neurology* 8: 306.

Myrick, H., R. F. Anton, X. Li, S. Henderson, P. K. Randall, and K. Voronin. 2008. "Effect of Naltrexone and Ondansetron on Alcohol Cue-Induced Activation of the Ventral Striatum in Alcohol-Dependent People." *Archives of General Psychiatry* 65 (4): 466–75.

Nestle, Marion. 2021. "Episode 34: Marion Nestle," in *Food Junkies Podcast*, August 19, 2021. 0:52, https://www.foodjunkiespodcast.com/episodes/episode-34-marion-nestle.

Nilson, E. A. F., G. Ferrari, M. L. C. Louzada, R. B. Levy, C. A. Monteiro, and L. F. M. Rezende. 2023. "Premature Deaths Attributable to the Consumption of Ultraprocessed Foods in Brazil." *American Journal of Preventive Medicine* 64 (1): 129–136.

Nilson, E. A. F., G. Ferrari, M. L. D. C. Louzada, R. B. Levy, C. A. Monteiro, and L. F. M. Rezende. 2022. "The Estimated Burden of Ultra-Processed Foods on Cardiovascular Disease Outcomes in Brazil: A Modeling Study." *Frontiers in Nutrition* 9: 1043620.

Ojalehto Lindfors, E., T. L. De Oliveira, C. A. Reynolds, Y. Zhan, A. K. Dahl Aslan, J. Jylhava, A. Sjölander, and I. K. Karlsson. 2024. "Genetic Influences, Lifestyle and Psychosocial Aspects in Relation to Metabolically Healthy Obesity and Conversion to a Metabolically Unhealthy State." *Diabetes, Obesity and Metabolism* 27 (1): 207–214.

Olszewski, P. K., A. Klockars, A. M. Olszewska, R. Fredriksson, H. B. Schioth, and A. S. Levine. 2010. "Molecular, Immunohistochemical, and Pharmacological Evidence of Oxytocin's Role as Inhibitor of Carbohydrate but Not Fat Intake." *Endocrinology* 151 (10): 4736–4744.

Opie, R. S., A. O'Neil, F. N. Jacka, J. Pizzinga, and C. Itsiopoulos. 2018. "A Modified Mediterranean Dietary Intervention for Adults with Major Depression: Dietary Protocol and Feasibility Data from the SMILES Trial." *Nutritional Neuroscience* 21 (7): 487–501.

Ouwens, M. A., T. van Strien, and J. F. van Leeuwe. 2009. "Possible Pathways Between Depression, Emotional and External Eating. A Structural Equation Model." *Appetite* 53 (2): 245–248.

Parnarouskis, L., E. M. Schulte, J. C. Lumeng, and A. N. Gearhardt. 2020. "Development of the Highly Processed Food Withdrawal Scale for Children." *Appetite* 147: 104553.

Pastor, V., and J. H. Medina. 2021. "Medial Prefrontal Cortical Control of Reward- and Aversion-Based Behavioral Output: Bottom-Up Modulation." *European Journal of Neuroscience* 53 (9): 3039–3062.

Pedram, P., D. Wadden, P. Amini, W. Gulliver, E. Randell, F. Cahill et al. 2013. "Food Addiction: Its Prevalence and Significant Association with Obesity in the General Population." *PLoS One* 8 (9): e74832.

Peirce Thompson, S. 2022. "Episode 80: Susan Pierce Thompson," in *Food Junkies Podcast*, July 7, 2022. 1:00, https://www.foodjunkiespodcast.com/episodes/episode-80-dr-susan-peirce-thompson.

Peng-Li, D., T. A. Sørensen, Y. Li, and Q. He. 2020. "Systematically Lower Structural Brain Connectivity in Individuals with Elevated Food Addiction Symptoms." *Appetite* 155: 104850.

Perry, C., T. S. Guillory, and S. S. Dilks. 2021. "Obesity and Psychiatric Disorders." *Nursing Clinics of North America* 56 (4): 553–563.

Peuhkuri, K., N. Sihvola, and R. Korpela. 2011. "Dietary Proteins and Food-Related Reward Signals." *Food and Nutrition Research* 55.

Pond, R. S., Jr., T. B. Kashdan, C. N. DeWall, A. Savostyanova, N. M. Lambert, and F. D. Fincham. 2012. "Emotion Differentiation Moderates Aggressive Tendencies in Angry People: A Daily Diary Analysis." *Emotion* 12 (2): 326–337.

Prnjak, K., D. Mitchison, S. Griffiths, J. Mond, N. Gideon, L. Serpell, and P. Hay. 2020. "Further Development of the 12-Item EDE-QS: Identifying a Cut-Off for Screening Purposes." *BMC Psychiatry* 20 (1): 146.

Pursey, K. M., P. Stanwell, A. N. Gearhardt, C. E. Collins, and T. L. Burrows. 2014. "The Prevalence of Food Addiction as Assessed by the Yale Food Addiction Scale: A Systematic Review." *Nutrients* 6 (10): 4552–4590.

References

Reichelt, A. C., S. Killcross, L. D. Hambly, M. J. Morris, and R. F. Westbrook. 2015. "Impact of Adolescent Sucrose Access on Cognitive Control, Recognition Memory, and Parvalbumin Immunoreactivity." *Learning and Memory* 22 (4): 215–224.

Reichelt, A. 2023. "Episode 143: Dr. Amy Reichelt, PhD," in *Food Junkies Podcast*, September 21, 2023. 1:15, https://www.foodjunkiespodcast.com/episodes/episode-143-dr-amy-reichelt-phd.

Reichenbach, A., R. E. Clarke, R. Stark, S. H. Lockie, M. Mequinion, H. Dempsey et al. 2022. "Metabolic Sensing in Agrp Neurons Integrates Homeostatic State with Dopamine Signalling in the Striatum." *Elife* 11: e72668.

Robertson, C. L., K. Ishibashi, J. Chudzynski, L. J. Mooney, R. A. Rawson, B. A. Dolezal, C. B. Cooper, A. K. Brown, M. A. Mandelkern, and E. D. London. 2015. "Effect of Exercise Training on Striatal Dopamine D2/D3 Receptors in Methamphetamine Users during Behavioral Treatment." *Neuropsychopharmacology* 41 (6): 1629–1636.

Rostanzo, E., M. Marchetti, I. Casini, and A. M. Aloisi. 2021. "Very-Low-Calorie Ketogenic Diet: A Potential Treatment for Binge Eating and Food Addiction Symptoms in Women. A Pilot Study." *International Journal of Environmental Research and Public Health* 18 (23): 12802.

Samakidou, G. E., C. C. Koliaki, E. N. Liberopoulos, and N. L. Katsilambros. 2023. "Non-Classical Aspects of Obesity Pathogenesis and Their Relative Clinical Importance for Obesity Treatment." *Healthcare* 11 (9): 1310.

Sarkar, S., K. P. Kochhar, and N. A. Khan. 2019. "Fat Addiction: Psychological and Physiological Trajectory." *Nutrients* 11 (11): 2785.

Schienle, A., I. Unger, and A. Wabnegger. 2020. "Comparison of Women with High Vs. Low Food Addiction Tendency: A Pilot Study with Voxel-Based Morphometry." *Journal of Eating Disorders* 8: 13.

Schuch, F. B., D. Vancampfort, J. Richards, S. Rosenbaum, P. B. Ward, and B. Stubbs. 2016. "Exercise As A Treatment For Depression: A Meta-Analysis Adjusting For Publication Bias." *Journal of Psychiatric Research* 77: 42–51.

Schulte, E. M. 2022. "Episode 85: Dr. Erica Schulte, Ph.D.," in *Food Junkies Podcast*, August 10, 2022. 1:04, https://www.foodjunkiespodcast.com/episodes/episode-85-drerica-schulte-phd.

Schulte, E. M., N. M. Avena, and A. N. Gearhardt. 2015. "Which Foods May Be Addictive? The Roles of Processing, Fat Content, and Glycemic Load." *PLoS One* 10 (2): e0117959.

Schulte, E. M., and A. N. Gearhardt. 2017. "Development of the Modified Yale Food Addiction Scale Version 2.0." *European Eating Disorders Review* 25 (4): 302–308.

Schulte, E. M., T. V. E. Kral, and K. C. Allison. 2022. "A Cross-Sectional Examination of Reported Changes to Weight, Eating, and Activity Behaviors During the COVID-19 Pandemic Among United States Adults with Food Addiction." *Appetite* 168: 105740.

Schulte, E. M., J. K. Smeal, J. Lewis, and A. N. Gearhardt. 2018. "Development of the Highly Processed Food Withdrawal Scale." *Appetite* 131: 148–154.

Sehrig, S., M. Odenwald, and B. Rockstroh. 2021. "Feedback-Related Brain Potentials Indicate the Influence of Craving on Decision-Making in Patients with Alcohol Use Disorder: An Experimental Study." *European Addiction Research* 27 (3): 216–226.

Serralde-Zuñiga, A. E., A. G. González-Garay, Y. Rodríguez-Carmona, and G. Meléndez-Mier. 2022. "Use of Fluoxetine to Reduce Weight in Adults with Overweight or Obesity: Abridged Republication of the Cochrane Systematic Review." *Obesity Facts* 15 (4): 473–486.

Sketriene, D., D. Battista, L. Lalert, N. Kraiwattanapirom, H. N. Thai, T. Leeboonngam et al. 2022. "Compulsive-Like Eating of High-Fat High-Sugar Food is Associated with 'Addiction-Like' Glutamatergic Dysfunction in Obesity Prone Rats." *Addiction Biology* 27 (5): e13206.

Skinner, J. A., M. Leary, M. Whatnall, R. A. Collins, K. M. Pursey, A. Verdejo-Garcia et al. 2024. "A Three-Arm Randomised Controlled Trial of a Telehealth Intervention Targeting Improvement in Addictive Eating for Australian Adults (The TRACE Program)." *Appetite* 195: 107211.

Staudacher, H. M., S. Mahoney, K. Canale, R. S. Opie, A. Loughman, D. So, L. Beswick, C. Hair, and F. N. Jacka. 2024. "Clinical Trial: A Mediterranean Diet is Feasible and Improves Gastrointestinal and Psychological Symptoms in Irritable Bowel Syndrome." *Alimentary Pharmacology and Therapeutics* 59 (4): 492–503.

Stelly, C. E., S. C. Tritley, Y. Rafati, and M. J. Wanat. 2020. "Acute Stress Enhances Associative Learning via Dopamine Signaling in the Ventral Lateral Striatum." *Journal of Neuroscience* 40 (22): 4391-4400.

Tabri, Nassim. 2023. "Episode 144: Dr. Nassim Tabri, PhD," in *Food Junkies Podcast*, September 27, 2023. 1:00, https://www.foodjunkiespodcast.com/episodes/episode-144-dr-nassim-tabri-phd.

Tarman, V. 2024. "One Size Does Not Fit All: Understanding the Five Stages of Ultra-Processed Food Addiction." *Journal of Metabolic Health* 7 (1).

———. 2019. *Food Junkies: Recovery from Food Addiction*. 2nd ed. Toronto: Dundurn Press.

Tasali, E., K. Wroblewski, E. Kahn, J. Kilkus, and D. A. Schoeller. 2022. "Effect of Sleep Extension on Objectively Assessed Energy Intake Among Adults With Overweight in Real-life Settings: A Randomized Clinical Trial." *JAMA Internal Medicine* 182 (4): 365–374.

Taubes, G. 2021. "Episode 30: Gary Taubes," July 22, 2021. 0:49, https://www.foodjunkiespodcast.com/episodes/episode-gary-taubes.

Teicholz, N. 2023. "Episode 148: Nina Teicholz," in *Food Junkies Podcast*, October 26, 2023. 0:51, https://www.foodjunkiespodcast.com/episodes/episode-148-nina-teicholz.

Trauer, J. M., M. Y. Qian, J. S. Doyle, S. M. W. Rajaratnam, and D. Cunnington. 2015. "Cognitive Behavioral Therapy for Chronic Insomnia: A Systematic Review and Meta-Analysis." *Annals of Internal Medicine* 163 (3): 191–204.

Unwin, D. 2021a. "Episode 45: Dr. David Unwin," in *Food Junkies Podcast*, October 28, 2021. 0:53, https://www.foodjunkiespodcast.com/episodes/episode-45-dr-david-unwin.

Unwin, J., C. Delon, H. Giaever, C. Kennedy, M. Painschab, F. Sandin, C. S. Poulsen, and D. A. Wiss. 2022. "Low Carbohydrate And Psychoeducational Programs Show Promise for the Treatment of Ultra-Processed Food Addiction." *Frontiers in Psychiatry* 13: 1005523.

Unwin, J., H. Giaever, M. Painschab, and C. Kennedy. 2024. "Episode 175: International Food Addiction Consensus Conference," in *Food Junkies Podcast*, May 2, 2024. 0:47, https://www.foodjunkiespodcast.com/episodes/episode-175-international-food-addiction-consensus-conference.

References

Unwin, J. 2021b. "Episode 11: Dr. Jen Unwin," in *Food Junkies Podcast*, March 11, 2021. 0:57, https://www.foodjunkiespodcast.com/episodes/episode-11-dr-jen-unwin.

Van Rensburg, K. J., A. Taylor, and T. Hodgson. 2009. "The Effects of Acute Exercise on Attentional Bias Towards Smoking-Related Stimuli During Temporary Abstinence from Smoking." *Addiction* 104 (11): 1910–1917.

Van Tulleken, Chris. 2023. "Episode 156: Dr. Chris Van Tulleken," in *Food Junkies Podcast*, December 21, 2023. 0:53, https://www.foodjunkiespodcast.com/episodes/episode-156-dr-chris-van-tulleken.

Vanderschuren, L. J., P. Di Ciano, and B. J. Everitt. 2005. "Involvement of the Dorsal Striatum in Cue-Controlled Cocaine Seeking." *Journal of Neuroscience* 25 (38): 8665–8670.

Volkow, N. D., G.J. Wang, L. Maynard, J. S. Fowler, B. Jayne, F. Telang et al. 2002. "Effects of Alcohol Detoxification on Dopamine D2 Receptors in Alcoholics: A Preliminary Study." *Psychiatry Research-Neuroimaging* 116 (3): 163–172.

Volkow, N. D., L. Chang, G. J. Wang, J. S. Fowler, D. Franceschi, M. Sedler et al. 2001. "Loss of Dopamine Transporters in Methamphetamine Abusers Recovers with Protracted Abstinence." *Journal of Neuroscience* 21 (23): 9414–9418.

Vora, E. 2022. "Episode 100: Dr. Ellen Vora, MD," in *Food Junkies Podcast*, November 24, 2022. 0:57, https://www.foodjunkiespodcast.com/episodes/episode-100-dr-ellen-vora-md.

Walker, B. M. 2012. "Conceptualizing Withdrawal-Induced Escalation of Alcohol Self-Administration as a Learned, Plasticity-Dependent Process." *Alcohol* 46 (4): 339–348.

Wang, D., C. Zhou, and Y. K. Chang. 2015. "Acute Exercise Ameliorates Craving and Inhibitory Deficits in Methamphetamine: An ERP Study." *Physiology and Behavior* 147: 38–46.

Wang, G. J., D. Tomasi, N. D. Volkow, R. Wang, F. Telang, E. C. Caparelli, and E. Dunayevich. 2014. "Effect of Combined Naltrexone and Bupropion Therapy on the Brain's Reactivity to Food Cues." *International Journal of Obesity* 38 (5): 682–688.

Ward, Z. J., S. N. Bleich, M. W. Long, and S. L. Gortmaker. 2021. "Association of Body Mass Index with Health Care Expenditures in the United States by Age and Sex." *PLoS One* 16 (3): e0247307.

Ward, Z. J., W. C. Willett, F. B. Hu, L. S. Pacheco, M. W. Long, and S. L. Gortmaker. 2022. "Excess Mortality Associated with Elevated Body Weight in the USA by State and Demographic Subgroup: A Modelling Study." *eClinicalMedicine* 48: 101429.

Werdell, Phil. 2022. "Episode 69: Phil Werdell & Mary Foushi," in *Food Junkies Podcast*, April 19, 2022. 0:57, https://www.foodjunkiespodcast.com/episodes/episode-69-phil-werdell-amp-mary-foushi.

Westman, Eric. 2021. "Episode 47: Dr. Eric Westman," in *Food Junkies Podcast*, November 15, 2021. 0:55, https://www.foodjunkiespodcast.com/episodes/episode-47-dr-eric-westman.

Wetherill, R. R., N. Spilka, K. Jagannathan, P. Morris, D. Romer, T. Pond, K. G. Lynch, T. R. Franklin, and H. R. Kranzler. 2021. "Effects Of Topiramate on Neural Responses to Alcohol Cues in Treatment-Seeking Individuals with Alcohol Use Disorder: Preliminary Findings from a Randomized, Placebo-Controlled Trial." *Neuropsychopharmacology* 46 (8): 1414–1420.

Wilcox, C. 2021. *Food Addiction, Obesity and Disorders of Overeating: An Evidence-Based Asessment and Clinical Guide*. Cham, Switzerland: Springer International.

Wilcox, C. E., C. C. Abbott, and V. D. Calhoun. 2019. "Alterations in Resting-State Functional Connectivity in Substance Use Disorders and Treatment Implications." *Progress in Neuropsychopharmacology and Biological Psychiatry* 91: 79–93.

Wilcox, C. E., C. J. Dekonenko, A. R. Mayer, M. P. Bogenschutz, and J. A. Turner. 2014. "Cognitive Control in Alcohol Use Disorder: Deficits and Clinical Relevance." *Reviews in Neuroscience* 25 (1): 1–24.

Wilcox, C. E., M. R. Pearson, and J. S. Tonigan. 2015. "Effects of Long-Term AA Attendance and Spirituality on the Course of Depressive Symptoms in Individuals with Alcohol Use Disorder." *Psychology of Addictive Behaviors* 29 (2): 382–391.

Wilcox, C. E., J. M. Pommy, and B. Adinoff. 2016. "Neural Circuitry of Impaired Emotion Regulation in Substance Use Disorders." *American Journal of Psychiatry* 173 (4): 344–361.

Wilcox, C. E., and J. S. Tonigan. 2018. "Changes in Depression Mediate the Effects of AA Attendance on Alcohol Use Outcomes." *American Journal of Drug and Alcohol Abuse* 44 (1): 103–112.

Wilcox, C.E., M.N. Braskie, J.T. Kluth, and W. J. Jagust. 2010. "Overeating Behavior and Striatal Dopamine with 6-[18F]-Fluoro-L-m-Tyrosine PET." *Journal of Obesity*.

Wiss, D. 2021a. "Episode 2: Interview with David Wiss," in *Food Junkies Podcast*, January 6, 2021. 0:53, https://www.foodjunkiespodcast.com/episodes/episode-02-davidwiss.

———. 2021b. "Episode 31: David Wiss," in *Food Junkies Podcast*, July 29, 2021. 0:53, https://www.foodjunkiespodcast.com/episodes/episode-31-david-wiss.

———. 2022a. "Clinical Considerations of Ultra-processed Food Addiction Across Weight Classes: An Eating Disorder Treatment and Care Perspective." *Current Addiction Reports* 9 (4): 255–267.

———. 2022b. "Episode 88: Dr. David Wiss, Ph.D.," in *Food Junkies Podcast*, August 31, 2022. 0:56, https://www.foodjunkiespodcast.com/episodes/episode-88-dr-david-wiss-phd.

———. 2023. "Episode 150: Dr. David Wiss," in *Food Junkies Podcast*, November 09, 2023 1:01, https://www.foodjunkiespodcast.com/episodes/episode-150-dr-david-wiss.

Wiss, D., and T. Brewerton. 2020. "Separating the Signal from the Noise: How Psychiatric Diagnoses Can Help Discern Food Addiction from Dietary Restraint." *Nutrients* 12 (10): 2937.

Yang, Allie. 2022. "How Sugar and Fat Affect Your Brain." *National Geographic*, December 28, 2022. https://www.nationalgeographic.com/magazine/article/how-sugar-and-fat-affect-your-brain.

Yang, Z., D. J. Oathes, K. A. Linn, S. E. Bruce, T. D. Satterthwaite, P. A. Cook, E. K. Satchell, H. Shou, and Y. I. Sheline. 2018. "Cognitive Behavioral Therapy Is Associated With Enhanced Cognitive Control Network Activity in Major Depression and Posttraumatic Stress Disorder." *Biological Psychiatry Cognitive Neuroscience and Neuroimaging* 3 (4): 311–319.

Zhao, L. Y., J. Tian, W. Wang, W. Qin, J. Shi, Q. Li et al. 2012. "The Role of Dorsal Anterior Cingulate Cortex in the Regulation of Craving by Reappraisal in Smokers." *PLoS One* 7 (8): e43598.

Claire Wilcox, MD, is a board-certified psychiatrist and addiction psychiatrist, associate professor of translational neuroscience at the Mind Research Network, frequent guest on the *Food Junkies* podcast, and adjunct faculty at the University of New Mexico. She has worked in a variety of clinical settings, including a medical weight loss clinic and an eating disorder treatment facility, and she completed an internal medicine residency before her psychiatry residency. She has been awarded National Institutes of Health (NIH) grants for her research in addiction neuroscience, and has published numerous academic works, including a textbook on food addiction titled *Food Addiction, Obesity, and Disorders of Overeating*. She was associate editor of the *New England Journal of Medicine Journal Watch* from 2017-2020, blogs regularly on *Psychology Today*, and has written for *Santa Fe Reporter* and *Science in the News*, among others.

Foreword writer **Clarissa Kennedy, RSW**, is a clinical social worker and addiction recovery specialist with more than fifteen years of experience helping individuals and families navigate food addiction and eating disorders. Her personal recovery journey informs her compassionate approach, fostering trust and understanding with clients.

Foreword writer **Molly Painschab, LCPC**, is a licensed clinical professional counselor, nationally certified counselor, and expert in addiction recovery with a special focus on food addiction and its intersection with trauma and mental health. Painschab is cofounder of Sweet Sobriety, where she empowers individuals to overcome challenges associated with ultra-processed food addiction and cultivate healthier, more fulfilling lives.

Foreword writer **Vera Tarman** is author of *Food Junkies*, and medical director of Renascent. She is also cohost of the successful *Food Junkies* podcast, along with Molly Painschab and Clarissa Kennedy. You can also find her on her free Facebook group, "I'm Sweet Enough: Sugar-Free for Life," and her YouTube channel: Veratarmanmd.

Real change *is* possible

For more than fifty years, New Harbinger has published proven-effective self-help books and pioneering workbooks to help readers of all ages and backgrounds improve mental health and well-being, and achieve lasting personal growth. In addition, our spirituality books offer profound guidance for deepening awareness and cultivating healing, self-discovery, and fulfillment.

Founded by psychologist Matthew McKay and Patrick Fanning, New Harbinger is proud to be an independent, employee-owned company. Our books reflect our core values of integrity, innovation, commitment, sustainability, compassion, and trust. Written by leaders in the field and recommended by therapists worldwide, New Harbinger books are practical, accessible, and provide real tools for real change.

MORE BOOKS from NEW HARBINGER PUBLICATIONS

THE INTUITIVE EATING WORKBOOK, SECOND EDITION

Ten Principles for Nourishing a Healthy Relationship with Food

978-1648484599 / US $26.95

SIMPLE WAYS TO UNWIND WITHOUT ALCOHOL

50 Tips to Drink Less and Enjoy More

978-1648482342 / US $18.95

THE EMOTIONALLY EXHAUSTED WOMAN

Why You're Feeling Depleted and How to Get What You Need

978-1648480157 / US $20.95

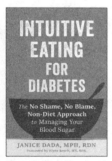

INTUITIVE EATING FOR DIABETES

The No Shame, No Blame, Non-Diet Approach to Managing Your Blood Sugar

978-1648484094 / US $19.95

THE STRESS-PROOF BRAIN GUIDED JOURNAL

Writing Practices to Rewire Your Emotional Response to Stress and Feel Calm

978-1648481680 / US $18.95

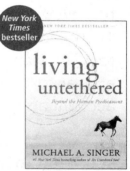

LIVING UNTETHERED

Beyond the Human Predicament

978-1648480935 / US $18.95

newharbingerpublications

1-800-748-6273 / newharbinger.com

(VISA, MC, AMEX / prices subject to change without notice)

Follow Us

Don't miss out on new books from New Harbinger.
Subscribe to our email list at **newharbinger.com/subscribe**

Did you know there are **free tools** you can download for this book?

Free tools are things like **worksheets, guided meditation exercises**, and **more** that will help you get the most out of your book.

You can download free tools for this book—whether you bought or borrowed it, in any format, from any source—from the New Harbinger website. All you need is a NewHarbinger.com account. Just use the URL provided in this book to view the free tools that are available for it. Then, click on the "download" button for the free tool you want, and follow the prompts that appear to log in to your NewHarbinger.com account and download the material.

You can also save the free tools for this book to your **Free Tools Library** so you can access them again anytime, just by logging in to your account! Just look for this button on the book's free tools page.

+ Save this to my free tools library

If you need help accessing or downloading free tools, visit **newharbinger.com/faq** or contact us at **customerservice@newharbinger.com**.